TRANSFORMATIONAL LEADERSHIP
SHARED DREAMS TO SUCCEED

Transformational Leadership
Shared Dreams to Succeed

Alain Godard and Vincent Lenhardt
Foreword by Jean-René Fourtou

palgrave

The original French edition of this book was published as
Engagements, Espoirs, Rêves by Alain Godard and Vincent
Lenhardt, published by Village Mondial, Paris.

This edition published 2000 by
PALGRAVE
Houndmills, Basingstoke, Hampshire RG21 6XS and
175 Fifth Avenue, New York, NY 10010
Companies and representatives throughout the world.

PALGRAVE is the new global academic imprint of
St. Martin's Press LLC Scholarly and Reference Division and
Palgrave Publishers Ltd (formerly Macmillan Press Ltd).

ISBN 0–333–92899–7

This book is printed on paper suitable for recycling and
made from fully managed and sustained forest sources.

A catalogue record for this book is available
from the British Library.

Library of Congress Cataloging-in-Publication Data

Godard, Alain, 1946–
  [Engagements, espoirs, rêves. English]
    Transformational leadership : shared dreams to succeed / by
  Alain Godard and Vincent Lenhardt ; foreword by Jean-René Fourtou.
      p. cm.
    Translation of: Engagements, espoirs, rêves.
    Includes bibliographical references and index.
    ISBN 0–333–92899–7
    1. Leadership.   I. Lenhardt, Vincent. II. Title.
HD57.7 .G6313 2000
658.4'092—dc21   00-062603

10   9   8   7   6   5   4   3   2   1
09   08   07   06   05   04   03   02   01   00

Design and page make-up by *Ascenders*

Printed in Great Britain by
Creative Print & Design (Wales), Ebbw Vale.

Contents

PART 3
The Present and The Future

Acknowledgement

We should particularly like to thank the following persons for their aid and support in the preparation and checking of the typescript: Ismahane Askri, Anne-Marie Burellier, Hélène Darmon, Rossella Daverio, Francine Godard, Nathalie Godard, Jean-Loup de Lamotte and Dominique Olivaux.

Alain Godard
Vincent Lenhardt

Introduction to the English Edition

This book was originally written in French, during the summer of 1998. Today we are truly delighted to see it translated into English and printed by a publishing house as well regarded as Palgrave. We both have a very particular affection for the story told in the following pages, and the lessons we draw from it. Thus, we are very pleased to make it available to a larger international audience.

This story started in 1993 and came to an end – at least the end of its first and most difficult stage – in 1997. This means that it is an old story if one looks at the current pace of evolution, progress and change. Actually, many things have also changed within the company where the experiences related in this book took place. This company now has a new name, a new shareholding asset, a larger dimension and a more focussed scope. However, we are convinced that the lessons we learned are still very young. They are all about increasing complexity, market challenges, hard competition, bad performance, cultural revolutions and then … 'the light at the end of the tunnel'. And, more importantly, they are about the unbelievable level of talent, creativity and solidarity that human beings can show in the middle of a storm, provided they can openly share information and goals, fears and courage, and, above all, a common language and a common vision – or, as we like to say, common dreams.

In our view, the most original part of our story is the proof that one can successfully combine economic and social concerns, focus on the bottom line and care for people. Often considered as a paradox, such a combination can produce long-lasting success much more than the traditional 'layoff solution'. To practise paradoxes is probably the only way to cope with complexity.

Another original aspect that we like to underline is the combination of the two of us – a paradox again. One of us is a corporate executive, with a long experience of very operational management, used to taking 'hard' decisions every day and being evaluated mainly on his economic performance year after year. The other one has been for many years a psychotherapist and a teacher in transactional analysis, as well as a consultant in coaching and team building: all very 'soft' competencies.

We think that our main commonalities can be summarized into two points: we have both an international experience and a multicultural approach, and we both believe in respect for people. This is why we are able to co-operate quite positively, including in writing this book. Because of our differences, the book combines practice and theory – concrete actions and the theoretical parameters that are behind them. We explain how to manage difficulties and complexity through the enhancement of the 'collective intelligence' of an entire organization. We think that this assumption is still very valuable, and it will be even more in the future.

We hope you can find in this book some useful suggestion and captivating inspiration.

Alain Godard
Vincent Lenhardt

Foreword

One must take every opportunity to repeat that the lasting success of a company is above all based on people. What counts is their motivation, their will to work together, their capacity to define and share in a project which gives meaning to their efforts, their professionalism and their imagination.

Apart from being the account of an exemplary adventure, this book is also the fruit of a shared reflection between a corporate executive, Alain Godard, and a consultant, Vincent Lenhardt. What lessons can be drawn from this experience with regard to current and future management trends? How can our managers of tomorrow and our organizations be better prepared in this environment of uncertainty and complexity?

The second part of the book, and the third more conceptual part, describe a number of key situations that we must face, and adopt an approach that is especially dear to me, namely the empowerment of everyone in what is referred to as the 'polycellular company' and the logic of 'subsidiarity'.

Management teams are like sports teams. They enjoy periods of excitement when they overcome obstacles together, surpass themselves, and turn around situations which at the start seemed hopeless. But industrial life is such that these same teams also experience gloomy periods, when the course of events goes in the wrong direction, when bad luck intervenes and doubt invades. And as with sport, it is in adversity that great teams show themselves.

This book describes the leap, and the safe landing, undertaken by the Agro team of Rhône-Poulenc when in 1993 it was confronted with a drastic fall in the market, a collapse in its financial performance and the anxiety and doubt which were quick to follow.

The team itself had been formed at the end of 1986 at the time of the merger between Rhône-Poulenc Agro and Union Carbide Agrochemicals, the Group's first large-scale acquisition in the United States. This operation bore great risks: Union Carbide sold the business 'on the books' and the two teams did not know each other. Furthermore, our experience of this type of industrial merger, which was both transatlantic and global, was extremely limited.

Under the leadership of Philippe Desmarescaux and Alain Godard, after a year of uncertainty and relentless work, there emerged the Group's first truly global team, with a new culture, offshoots in all continents, an international management, great ambition and results that were to see regular growth. Then, in 1993 came the crises, both economic and in the European agricultural market. Where did this team find itself, seven years after the merger that had created it? What were its inner reserves, its vital energy and its qualities of imagination and response?

Two years previously, on the recommendation of Philippe Desmarescaux, Alain Godard had been appointed Chief Executive Officer. How would he face up to adversity? How would he withstand the loss of confidence and legitimacy which unfortunately but inevitably develops insidiously in such circumstances? How would he set his pace in the crowd of gossips and with too many suggestions coming from everyone?

There was a strong temptation to apply energetically a course of action already known and well mastered by the Group from the problem that we had had in textiles and heavy chemicals, namely substantial restructuring to bring about a significant reduction in fixed costs. But, year on year, the Agro team had remained vigilant and had regularly increased productivity; action such as this would not alone bring salvation.

After a period of introspection and trial, Alain Godard opted for a bold gamble that was risky in these recessionary circumstances. By means of a cultural shock that aimed to mobilize everyone, empower the workplace, appeal to the imagination and intelligence of all, and within the framework of a clear project, he introduced a strict code of ethics and a simple but very efficient financial management system.

Success exceeded all hopes, with good fortune, as so often, finally lending support to the collective effort through the discovery of new products, followed by recovery in the market. Thanks to the SDM (Simplify, Decentralize, Manage) programme developed by Alain Godard and his teams, Agro has become a profitable business, with an excellent work environment, based on trust and solidarity, and with a rate of innovation among the most productive in the industry, both at the product level and in applications on the ground.

Could we have left it at that when science is at the start of a revolution whose consequences will be vast, world population is increasing and its needs are growing in quantity and quality, and globalization is causing powerful companies to emerge on a planetary scale?

Rhône-Poulenc decided to respond to this huge scientific, economic and social evolution by joining with Hoechst, another large European player in the sciences of agriculture and human health. This union has brought about the creation of Aventis, which has been in operation since the end of 1999 and whose ambition is to contribute, through its innovation, to the improvement of everyone's quality of life through the prevention of diseases, their therapeutic treatment and a better quality of food at more reasonable prices.

A merger of this scale between two large industrial groups, each rich in history, traditions and pride, represents at one and the same time a major advantage and a complex challenge, in which the human factor is primordial. Listening to and respecting others, opening up to different cultures, giving value to diversity and making it a source of creativity, facilitating dialogue and the exchange of knowledge, coming finally to share a common vision: these are the keys to true success. At Aventis we strive to put them into practice every day.

To manage such changes and give substance to these values, the leaders must above all be 'carriers of meaning' whose talents crystallize in the motivation of new teams and in a new company project.

Furthermore, their social awareness must enable the leaders to resolve the difficulties of those who are touched by these large movements of consolidation in an exemplary manner, that is, with clarity, generosity, availability and imagination.

In a globalized world, companies suffer from financial, technological, commercial and social pressures that are very intense and often conflicting. Change is permanent and the future is marked with opportunities but also with risks.

In the face of this, it is the values of men and women, teams and their leaders, their ability to adapt permanently to new situations and to think and behave 'differently', that constitute the cement of modern organizations and the most solid foundation for building a positive future.

This is the message of this original book, which harmoniously combines the account of the experience with conceptual reflection about the history of a 'humanistic success'.

Jean-René Fourtou
Vice-Chairman of Aventis
Former Chairman of Rhône-Poulenc
February 2000

Before Starting Our Journey

Meeting a 'principal witness'

At the beginning of 1997, when I had to organize and present a day's session on the theme 'Collective Intelligence and Effective Teams' for clients of the firm Transformance, I asked Alain Godard to participate as 'principal witness' to talk about his experience. From 1993 to 1996 he had in fact led a remarkable operation of change within Rhône-Poulenc Agro, of which he was Chief Executive Officer at the time.

Rhône-Poulenc Agro was one of the large subsidiaries of the Rhône-Poulenc Group specializing in crop protection, and at the time had a global turnover of FF10 bn, with nearly 7000 employees working in more than 60 affiliates spread through the five continents.

Being affected by the consequences of the Common Agricultural Policy (CAP) in 1993, the company saw its results collapse. Then Alain decided to launch operation SDM (Simplify, Decentralize, Manage) which enabled him to straighten out the business in the record time of two years, in a way that was not only effective in terms of financial results, but which used a thoroughly innovative approach. His remarkable achievement was to combine the human elements with the economic imperatives.

This success was quickly noticed both inside and outside the Group, and earned him his seat on the executive committee of Rhône-Poulenc in January 1997. He became chairman of the Plant and Animal Health Sector, embracing all activities of the Group associated with agriculture (a turnover of FF28 bn), before being entrusted at the beginning of 1998 with supervision of Asia for the entire activities of the Group.

Alain Godard came on the day organized by Transformance to describe his experience very simply to an audience of some thirty corporate executives and managers. Afterwards, I thought it would be really valuable if Alain were to write down the account of this experience so that the lessons that he had drawn from it might be shared. I therefore invited him to present a statement of whatever in this adventure could be, if not directly reproducible, at least a stimulus for executives and for agents of change directly involved with comparable responsibilities. It would also be of value for anyone involved in such a situation – shareholders, operational managers, union officials, the workforce of large and small companies, teachers and students who might one day be faced with similar problems. At this point I should also mention that the CEDEP – an organization close to the French management school INSEAD – published a case study on SDM, in English, which has been used by students in France and in the United States.

Alain hesitated for some time in the face of this proposal. Despite a taste for writing, he had never actually had occasion to tackle the blank page and was not sure that he would find the time to do it. Furthermore, his personality was such that it was not in his nature to push himself forward by describing an experience which he would consider as normal, and since I had worked with him for more than five years I was not surprised. I therefore proposed to do with him what I had recently done with another director, Bertrand Martin, former Chairman and Managing Director of Sulzer – the French subsidiary of the well-known Swiss group – which had been the task of 'decoding' a rather similar adventure.[1] This example was all the more appealing for Alain since he had spontaneously, and without informing me, circulated internally two pages from that document in order to illustrate his convictions on management. This choice showed and confirmed our profound agreement on core values.

Alain agreed to embark on the venture with me. It was a question of bearing witness without preaching, theorizing without lengthy jargon on subjects that were nonetheless complex and deep (crisis management, change, the profound dynamics of people and managerial development, the sociology of organizations, management and the new role of leaders, and so on), rooting the narrative in the real world and remaining sufficiently concise to be accessible to the busy manager.

The core of the book was conceived and written in the summer of 1998 involving some meetings and a lot of personal work from both of us. Though a co-authored work, this is above all the account of Alain Godard and his teams.

We knew each other sufficiently well to be mutually confident at the professional as well as the personal level. I first met Alain in 1992. He had asked me to help him and his executive committee which at the time had run into operational difficulties that were largely due to its multicultural makeup. I acted as coach at several team-building sessions and helped Alain in particular, going with him to the United States to better understand and improve his relations with the American members of the committee. This also enabled me to ensure the interface with the consultants in charge of quality policy, of which the Americans were fervent promoters and which had to be harmonized with the French approach. I also attended management briefing sessions at the start of the SDM operation, and subsequently, working with a Human Resources team, contributed to the framing of a management questionnaire that was to prove a determining tool for the implementation of common values and action principles throughout the organization. In 1994, I had the privilege of presenting the first session to introduce this tool, which implied the evaluation of Alain himself, carried out by his colleagues in his presence.

Apart from these specific interventions, I wish to state very clearly that I have no direct responsibility in the SDM operation and that it was led by Alain practically on his own and, as he stresses, without a consultant. This gave me a high level of freedom to discuss it, raise questions and underline certain key issues. My contribution to this book is mainly based on the fact that I acted rather as Alain's coach, helping him with my thoughts and questions to deliver his evidence and locate this adventure in the context of the most recent management theories and of numerous other operations of change in which I had participated or which I knew about from elsewhere.

Why is this adventure interesting?

- First because it is the story of a success. It is remarkable at the economic, human, organizational and managerial levels, while being based on calculated risks that are considerable in the face of the difficult conditions imposed by the context.
- Because Rhône-Poulenc Agro was a significant entity through its size, global position, and the complexity of its international and transcultural organization. Furthermore, the SDM experience follows on from a series of acquisitions, in particular of US companies with appreciably different cultures.
- Because this entity, significant though it is, was part of a larger international group – Rhône-Poulenc – itself little prepared for such an operation, despite the convictions of its Chairman Jean-René Fourtou.
- Because it is essentially the result of the political will and personal behaviour of an executive who is totally committed to the point of putting his job on the line.
- Because it is the result of drawing on the 'collective intelligence' of an organization in which almost everyone becomes progressively involved, employers and trades unions alike, all without any *a priori* aim of massive reductions in costs or employees. The quite limited social consequences of the operation were simply the result of 'creative co-evolution' (to borrow the expression of my associate and friend, Manfred Mack, author of a book[2] on the subject).
- Because in my opinion SDM illustrates magnificently an organized experience, drawing lessons from other experiences such as those described by Tom Peters, which so inspired Alain (the changes at ABB, General Electric, and so on), and introducing the approaches that emerged over time. These reveal the boundaries of 'management in complexity' in organizations that can no longer live solely according to the hierarchical and regulatory regimes of the past. They are irrevocably led to integrate into their approach to change – change of strategy, structures and systems – a process of empowerment of employees at all levels, and a permanent reconfiguration of the life of the organization carried out by these same players.
- Because it also illustrates a rare and remarkable alliance between the chairman of a large group – Jean-René Fourtou – and a large-scale operational executive – Alain Godard – that could serve as a model for all

our institutions large and small. In fact, Jean-René Fourtou, himself a former consultant and head of a large consultancy company (Bossard) before taking the helm of Rhône-Poulenc, had begun a movement in this direction by strongly encouraging his colleagues to decentralize, to introduce 'subsidiarity', networking and a polycellular management structure.[3] Alain in his account underlines the importance of having as chairman a person who allows and guarantees this type of initiative. Jean-René Fourtou also, with Alain, played the role of consultant, ambiguous though this may be, and facilitator, a role which, in my opinion, all company top managers should certainly learn.

- Finally, and above all, this account is important because in this post-industrial world, subject to chaos and uncertainty, to increasingly rapid changes, to short-term pressure from the financial world, and the temptations of managements to protect themselves by methods based mainly on control and reduction of costs and employees, Alain was able, courageously, to focus successfully on the fundamental stake of today's companies. In the face of all kinds of pressure (financial, technological, global, commercial, social, and so on) he took the risk of making a true 'refounding', not simply based on improving what existed, but on combining the short term with the long term, the economic with the human, the creation of value for the shareholder *and* for all participants, harnessing the living resources of the company and making them develop with him a new organization, a new management approach, thus allowing them to bring the values of the group into play. To summarize, he combined *value creation* in the broadest sense with the *implementation of values* in a recursive[4] dynamic conducted by the players themselves.

He was able to resist the temptation of wanting to solve the crisis by harsh measures that he had already practised, which are reassuring for the manager but often only correspond to the 'first curve treatment' – in the language of Charles Handy[5] – which marks the end of a functioning cycle. Alain was able to treat the 'second curve' at the same time – which corresponds to the reconfiguration of the whole system and which makes this operation a true refounding. Apart from the implementation of a new strategy, new structures and a new management identity, it aims at ensuring permanent renewal which is the only condition for the survival and growth of companies.

Organization of the book

We opted for a simple plan in which Alain Godard, after locating his experience in the internal context of Rhône-Poulenc and its environment, presents in Part 1 the SDM operation itself, together with his comments and personal memories.

Then, in Part 2, Alain discusses the lessons of his experience:

- How he saw and handled the fundamental issues.
- His analysis and explanation of various aspects of the operation.
- How he had been prepared by his personal and professional history to take such a situation in hand and make the choices he did.
- The management style that emerged from it.

Then, in Part 3, I attempt to outline thoughts on the present and the future for managers, on their organizations and their management, based on Alain's reflections and reactions on these topics.

To conclude, we try to reply to some questions, in particular the following:

- Is this experience reproducible?
- Does there need to be a crisis for such a radical approach to be adopted, or on the contrary must it be viewed as a procedure planned in advance?
- Are such thoughts reserved only for the managers of large international groups, or can they be useful to the owners of small businesses or even very small businesses?
- What advice would Alain give to those who would like to embark on such a venture?

Vincent Lenhardt

Notes

1 This resulted in the publication *Oser la Confiance* (Paris: Insep, 1996), produced in collaboration with Bruno Jarrosson and Bertrand Martin.

2 *Co-évolution, Dynamique Créatrice* (Paris: Village Mondial, 1997).

3 See Jean-René Fourtou and Jean-Christian Fauvet, *La Passion d'Entreprendre* (Paris: Les Éditions d'Organisation, 1985).

4 Recursive: the quality that produces the 'virtuous circle' in which the whole enriches the part, and *vice versa*.

5 Charles Handy, *Le Temps des Paradoxes* (Paris: Village Mondial, 1995), pp. 54–5.

A Real-life History

Alain Godard

RECONSTRUCTING the organization and its functioning principles from scratch had been the initial approach that led me to launch operation SDM (Simplify, Decentralize, Manage) based on strong but simple principles that I had stated from the beginning.

We had to get closer to our clients:

- Firstly, by defining:
  - a centre whose responsibilities would be limited to what was strictly necessary
  - decentralized units whose responsibilities would be enhanced.
- Secondly, by relying on strengthened management values and principles and on performance indicators suited to the priorities.
- Finally, by seeking a real change in behaviour among all company staff and an organization that favours cross-fertilizing projects.

These ideas formed the basis for the activities of the men and women who 'made' SDM, as they transformed these purely organizational elements into an extraordinary human adventure which I shall try to describe in the following pages.

I am often asked to come and talk about my experiences at teaching institutions, management clubs or outside firms concerned with the processes of change. On such occasions I have chosen to begin these presentations systematically by explaining three diagrams (Figures 1.1, 1.2 and 1.3) that show measurable results dealing with three different and complementary domains which, in my opinion, cannot be excluded from any assessment of the impact of change in an enterprise and in its lasting quality. They are:

1. *Finance/Economics*, the driving force of all companies, without which the remainder could not exist;
2. *Safety*, a key value for every activity based on an advanced technology that is constantly renewed and improved;
3. *Managerial behaviour*, something that is rarely measured, but which constitutes the 'compost' that helps tomorrow's people to grow, along with the innovations, the commitment and the success that will ensure the lasting quality of the company.

The financial/economic results

Figure 1.1 shows the evolution of the operational results (results after amortizations, before financial charges and taxes) and the return on capital

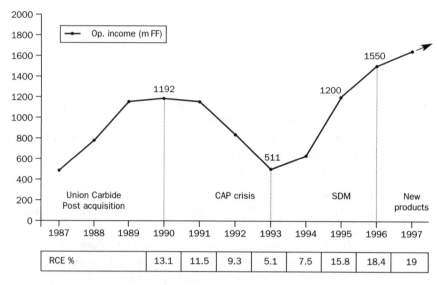

Figure 1.1 *Ten years of Rhône-Poulenc Agro*

employed (operational income/total capital employed) over a period of ten years (1986–96). We can identify four periods:

- 1987–1991: significant improvement associated with the acquisition and successful integration with the agrochemical activities of the American Union Carbide Company.
- 1992–1993: collapse of the company's financial performance, the main cause of which was the introduction of the European Common Agricultural Policy (CAP) bringing about a massive drop in the European agrochemical markets (–30 per cent).
- 1994–1996: rapid improvement in performance, due largely to the implementation of SDM, and supported by a stabilization of the markets, then a slight recovery at the end of the period.
- Post-1996: further period of improvement in performance due largely to the launch of new products developed during the preceding years. (The operational income of the Agro business was no longer published separately after 1997.)

We can see that the operational income of the company more than tripled between 1993 and 1996, whereas the turnover only increased by 13.6 per cent, and the research and development costs associated with the launch preparations of new products were significant. Even though some pick-up in the market (very limited compared with the earlier drop due to the CAP) did improve matters, and while 1993 and 1994 benefited from the impact of restructuring decisions made in 1992, we could legitimately claim that a large part of the improvement was associated with the implementation of operation SDM.

The safety results

I shall return later to the importance of values in a company in ensuring a true decentralization and a real empowerment of the players. Safety has long been identified as a key value for the whole of the Rhône-Poulenc Group. The simplest indicator used to measure advances in the area of safety is the IR1 (Incident Rate 1 which measures the number of industrial accidents with stoppages per million hours worked).

Figure 1.2 outlines the regular progress of the Group in this field but shows clearly the marked improvement of Rhône-Poulenc Agro from 1992; that is, during the economic crisis, then the improvement from SDM, achieving a new level in the middle of a period of change (1994).

These results, which appear at the highest level in a global bench-marking, are largely due to the tools and methods developed at Group level. But they show the acceleration that can be achieved through strong commitment from the managers, sustained during difficult and *a priori* destabilizing times such as those associated with economic difficulties and change.

Safety is from now on considered by everyone as 'his' or 'her' business, and the improvement has been sustained under the management of my successor on the executive committee of RP Agro (in 1998 the IR1 was less than 0.5).

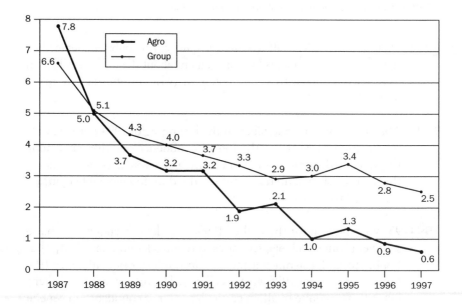

Figure 1.2 *Incident rate safety results of Rhône-Poulenc Agro and the Group*

Managerial behaviour

Because I was concerned to understand fully the company and its personnel, from 1992 I introduced a questionnaire, known as the 'social barometer', which allowed us to measure what the staff thought about the company, how it worked, and how it was managed, in France and in Europe (Figure 1.3).

Criteria	Year analysed	1992 (Start of 1993)	1993 (Start of 1994)	1994–95 (End of 1995)	1996 (Start of 1997)
Good company image		86	73	80	90
Optimistic about company		81	58	78	87
Confidence in top management		76	59	64	79
Generally motivated		71	61	66	77
Roles well defined		59	57	57	71
The client counts		83	79	88	95
Concern for profit		78	70	81	85
Senior management					
– knows how to listen		51	51	54	77
– knows how to decide		60	54	59	77
– knows how to delegate		62	59	57	74
Criteria averages		*70.7*	*62.1*	*68.4*	*81.2*

Figure 1.3 *Results of the social barometer enquiry at Rhône-Poulenc Agro between 1992 and 1997* (positive options shown as a percentage)

1992 Despite low results, staff remains optimistic, no doubt encouraged by the optimistic statements by management about the imminent launch of a new product with strong potential (which unfortunately never took off).

1993 The questionnaire undertaken at the beginning of 1994 in the middle of operation SDM shows the loss of confidence and disarray among the staff, both regarding the company and its management. Taking the average of the criteria measured, the drop in favourable opinions is from 70 to 62 per cent.

1994–95 We waited until the end of 1995 to make our enquiry so that a sufficient time had elapsed after the introduction of SDM, thus hoping to find a significant increase in the index of confidence (the financial results for 1995 were excellent). The figures show a recovery, but it remains quite small, in particular so far as confidence in general management and 'hierarchical' behaviour are concerned.

1996 It is during this year (the enquiry was made at the beginning of 1997) that the staff register that something has changed and say so: confidence in the company and in its management is at its highest level, but most of all, significant improvements are to be seen in the behaviour of senior management which are shown to know better how to *listen, decide* and *delegate*. This was one of the clear objectives sought by the decentralization, autonomy and empowerment implied in SDM. The results were equally good for the criterion of client priority which was the gateway for SDM (getting close to the client), and also good for role definition.

These results show, first of all, the relevance of a tool such as the social barometer which measures the underlying trends that are very useful for guiding work, the priorities and actions of management and of the human resources teams. From this example we can see how quickly staff confidence can evaporate, and the time it takes for it to be re-established; this is definitely a factor to be considered before any traumatizing decision if one believes in the importance of motivating men and women in the company to maximize financial/economic results. Finally, the results show that a real *change* has occurred during the period in the behaviour and perceptions of the entire social body of the company.

My reasons for presenting and commenting on these graphs before describing the sequence of events of operation SDM are firstly, to underline my strong conviction that one cannot measure the performance of a company simply in the light of its financial/economic (hereafter referred to as 'economic') results. I also wanted to try to make the reader aware that this experience, which forms the skeleton of this book, was for me and the staff an intense period, akin to a refounding. It was one of those unique occasions when one feels that groups of men and women are united in their energy to 'make possible what would appear rationally impossible', to borrow Bertrand Martin's fine expression[1].

1 Maturing

A growing fear ...

I was certainly preoccupied by the situation at the beginning of 1993. The European markets continued to fall, our new star product had run into a problem just as it was launched, and at the end of the day our financial results had collapsed.

This personal apprehension was greatly reinforced by the reactions of the Group's executive committee. I soon felt for the first time in my professional career a questioning that cast doubt on confidence in the Agro management team. To be frank, what emerged from a number of meetings held at the highest level towards the middle of 1993 was, from the Group chairman and the executive committee, the following question: 'Does this team, however likeable they may be, have the ability to turn the company around?'

Up until then I had enjoyed the complete confidence of my line managers in all my previous positions, and repeated successes had created for me the image of being a competent winner which I had held on to. I felt myself professionally called into question by this new situation and the solutions that were outlined – huge restructuring and a reduction in the portfolio of activities – seemed to me to be ill-suited to the state of affairs in this company which I knew well. For the past five years it had been subjected to restructuring and factory closures which had reduced the French employees by more than 35 per cent. It did not seem to me that the social body could tolerate more of this type of action which, moreover, did not appear likely to bring about the required improvement in the results (regain the previous level of profitability, that is to say an additional FF500 m of operational result). My initial concern thus turned into anxiety and then into a kind of fear for my colleagues and myself.

This unusual feeling played a major role in pushing me to react. At that moment I knew that I had to take the initiative and do something, rather like the soldier under attack who makes a sortie to avoid being overwhelmed. This marked the beginning of the maturing process, to which the beneficial pressure of the environment and my supervisors was not foreign. However, at this stage I had not the least idea of how I was going to start.

The emergence of a solution

In my conversations with Vincent Lenhardt he insists on the 'constructivist' nature of the SDM experience, a characteristic that he considers to be one of the major elements of management in uncertainty. In my case, several external elements came to catalyze my thoughts, leading me to the conviction that the outline solution should be based on three keywords: decentralization, empowerment and autonomy.

The first is the decentralization message stated repeatedly by Jean-René Fourtou for many years. As former chairman of Bossard Consultants, his thoughts on enterprises led him to want to turn a very centralized group into an organization that would rely on his convictions about the involvement of people and their empowerment. Up to that point his ideas had met with little response in the Group.

His message interested me, but because like everyone else I was bound up with day-to-day business and also enjoying a smooth-running career, I regarded it as a concept rather than a real solution. I would probably have left it at that if a second element had not intervened. In the middle of June 1993 I received a summary of the latest book by Tom Peters (*Liberation Management*); the contents were interesting and I bought the book. I read it from cover to cover, fascinated by the iconoclastic tone adopted for the judgement of 'classical' management and interested by the numerous examples and practical solutions supporting the argument. It was a hymn to decentralization and the building of a new company from scratch.

Reading this book confirmed my view that a solution was possible: I spent the summer thinking about it, beginning to imagine its spinal column, inspired by Tom Peters' suggestions and observations (see extract below). When at the beginning of September I explained to Philippe Desmarescaux and Jean-René Fourtou what I wanted to do, the latter replied: 'Go ahead, I prefer disorderly action to waiting and doing nothing ...' This remark galvanized the internal energy that I had built up in the summer.

Here are 39 strategies adapted from the 50 listed on pp 612–14 of *Liberation Management*.

The pursuit of luck: advice from Tom Peters

- Double and redouble the stakes. The more chances you take, the more chances you have.
- Get on with it. Enough of 'Shall I, shan't I'.
- Act.
- 'If a thing is worth doing, it is worth doing badly.' (G.K. Chesterton). At any rate, do something.
- Read odd stuff. Look anywhere for ideas.
- Make odd friends.
- Hire odd people.
- Work with odd partners.
- Delegate, empower. The more people around who are trying their luck, the more chance you have of doubling the stakes.
- Train without letting up. Train, without worrying about the production schedule. Train everyone, period.

- Pursue failure. Failure is the only route to success. The bigger the blunder, the more value it has.
- Arm yourself against the 'not-invented-here' syndrome that would only make you miss out on juicy ideas.
- Constantly reorganize. Mix, match, try different combinations to make things move.
- Listen to everyone. Ideas come from anywhere.
- Don't listen to anyone. Trust your inner ear.
- Nurture intuition. If you can find an interesting market idea that came from a rational plan, I'll eat *all* my hats (I have a collection).
- Don't hang out with 'all the rest'. Forget the same tired old trade association meetings, talking with the same tired people about the same tired things.
- Decentralize. Doubled stakes are proportional to the amount of decentralization.
- Decentralize again.
- Smash all functional barriers. Unfettered contact among people from different disciplines is magic.
- Destroy hierarchies.
- Open the books. Make everyone a 'business person', with access to all the financials.
- Start an information deluge. The more real-time, unedited information people close to the action have, the more that 'neat stuff' happens.
- Take sabbaticals.
- Spend 50 per cent of your time with 'outsiders'. Distributors and vendors will give you more ideas in five minutes than another five-hour committee meeting.
- Spread confusion in your wake. Keep people off balance, don't let the ruts get deeper than they already are.
- *Dis*organize. Bureaucracy takes care of itself. The boss must be the one to stop things going round in circles.
- *Dis*equilibrate. Create instability, even chaos.
- Stir curiosity. Igniting youthful, dormant curiosity in followers is the lead dog's top task, according to Sony chairman Akio Morita.
- Invent rewards for whoever attacks the company culture headlong. Look after these rare birds.
- Change your behaviour pattern. Vary your menus. Alter your daily movements.
- Take off your coat.
- Take off your tie.
- Roll up your sleeves.
- Take off your shoes.
- Get out of your office. Tell me, honestly, the last time something inspiring or clever happened at that big table in your office?
- Get rid of your office.
- Spend a workday each week at home.
- Avoid moderation in all things. Anything worth doing is worth doing to excess.

2 Ownership

The two circles

Another external event might have drawn my attention to the need for decentralization. The social barometer measuring 1992 was not bad (see again Figure 1.3, page 6), but it indicated a request from the staff on two topics: autonomy and the empowerment of hierarchies. At the time I had not seen a solution to these questions, being traditionally restricted to asking the human resources department to consider these problems and identify what action was needed.

It turns out that this approach played a fundamental role in the adopting of SDM, without my expecting it to. The Director of Human Resources, Jean-Paul Simmler, had convened a working party of some fifteen managers on the subject and had asked me to come along and exchange ideas on decentralization and management. The consulting firm 'Entreprise et Personnel' was in charge of moderating the debate.

Without having exactly planned this intervention, I exceeded their expectations in explaining the relatively revolutionary principles of what was to become SDM: elimination of the 'centre'[2], establishment of autonomous units managed by true entrepreneurs, freedom for those dealing directly with customers to choose any solution that brought a rapid increase in results. All these things called into question types of behaviour that were rooted in people's heads by years of practice that stifled all initiative, such as no recruitment without authorization, no price alterations or no advertising campaigns without agreement from the head office.

Their reaction was very favourable and was especially important for what followed; they represented the first circle of the initiated, they felt that what I had to tell them came from the guts and that I was going to carry the operation through with conviction, since I was ready to put my head on the block if things went wrong.

They not only repeated my proposals and so gave my approach credibility, they also rearranged their work in order to provide me a few days later with a note on what should and should not be done to make the project succeed. SDM owes much to them and I wish to record that here.

A short time after, in a more classic manner, I assembled my executive committee and presented my ideas, now relatively structured in the form of some forty slides. All supported my approach, apart from one member whose training and experience made him impervious to any idea of decentralization. However, thanks to his loyalty, even he was able to play a fundamental role in the change after everything was fully explained.

This second circle backed me like the first on the fact that we had to carry out this project ourselves, without any consultant; it was to be 'our' affair. I shall return to this point later.

Cascading down

Then began the internal cascade, through an information process by which we had to create in people's minds the idea that we were embarking on something totally new, calling the existing situation into question and with the promise of leading to a complete renaissance of the company.

Being long convinced of the importance of verbal communication in the company, I had instituted since 1992 a monthly meeting with a hundred managers to comment on the company's position, its successes and difficulties and to reply to questions from the floor. This briefing, called 'flash-info', started at 11.00 am and was followed by a lunch to allow informal discussion, so useful for building interpersonal relations and resolving problems. I had decided to use the 14 September briefing to launch SDM.

Armed with the forty transparencies which my closest colleagues had helped to improve, I was able to put over a strong message that was close to being dramatic, finding the necessary tone and tension to make the audience react. From the outset I announced the change in approach and the ambitious financial objectives to be achieved within two years (Figure 1.4 below), while insisting that priority was to be given to clients. I indicated that in my opinion the new head office should not contain more than fifty people, as against the current total of more than four hundred.

Reading the content cold some five years later, it was solid and convincing. But what swung the project in the right direction and lent credibility to the 'culture shock' was the announcement that the annual October budgetary 'High Mass' was cancelled and replaced by three days of reflection on the implementation of SDM with the chief managers worldwide. Tom Peters' examples helped me to explain that establishing a budget or business plan – that is laying out figures – when one no longer understands what is happening in the market serves no purpose. The sacrosanct budgetary reference was eliminated and replaced by a 'fervent duty' to continually improve on the results of year 'SDM – 1', which became the only comparison used.

All of this ensured that this briefing achieved its objective of heightening people's awareness. The reaction from the unions also contributed to this awareness; hostile but explanatory leaflets were circulated. Disquiet increased to the point where a petition of several hundred names was organized to request that union representatives should participate in the management seminar planned for October. This concern, which I was later able to direct positively, showed an interest in the approach. But at the time I needed to mobilize my immediate management and the presence of the unions at this seminar would have prevented this; hence my refusal of this request. For three weeks, there was talk of nothing but SDM and the meeting of 18, 19 and 20 October, which was to be held in our seminar centre at Chazay d'Azergues, near Lyon.

Transparencies presented at the briefing of 14.09.93

A Fundamental Change of Approach

For several years a huge effort of reorganization/restructuring/cost reduction has been carried out continuously.

It has achieved the objectives set for each activity.

Reduction of fixed costs/Budget 1993: FF150 bn.

Reduction of fixed costs factories/Budget 1993: FF70 bn.

The opposing evolution of our market and competitive environment obliges us to go further if we wish to remain a major autonomous player in the world agrochemical market.

Only a fundamental change of approach appears capable of bringing new solutions suited to an environment that is increasingly unsettled.

Decentralization = getting closer to the client.

Decentralization Project

1. *Objectives*
   Create a new dynamic that allows us to achieve, while remaining in close proximity to our clients/markets, five profit points in two years (FF500 bn) and a significant improvement in our self-funding, so that after this period we move forward on sound bases in order to ensure the long-term development of our innovation.

2. *Directions*
   There are three key directions:
   Simplify
   Decentralize
   Manage (management principles)

3. *Organization principles*
   (a) Redefine the role of 'head office' limiting it to what is strictly necessary.
   (b) Transfer the remainder to decentralized units defined as the combination of:
   operating account + manager responsible.

This meeting at Chazay presented the role of ownership and investigation in ideal form. I invited the eighty participants from around the world not only to take on board the principles of decentralization that I was proposing, but also to deepen the analysis 'by going further' (another Tom Peters suggestion).

The work groups were remarkably fruitful and several organizational changes were suggested and introduced. Relieved to be focusing on a clear objective, everyone was behind me in confirming that the goal of gaining five profit points in two years was ambitious but achievable, because it was a matter of getting the company out of the rut and back on the track of growth and innovation to become a leader in the third millennium.

It was a success that allowed all to share this common vision and get into step with what had to be done. I have rarely found in my professional experience such a motivating spirit and desire to succeed.

The work methods

One of the seminar working groups had worked on this subject and had confirmed the proposed suggestion that we should follow the approach adopted in 1987 for the merger with Union Carbide. We were in fact in a very similar situation of having to redraw the contours of the company, even though the concept of the organization – decentralization – was different.

Many had been through the Union Carbide experience and felt confident in applying the same method, the relevant explanatory documents of which had been brought out for the occasion:

- Setting up 'work domains' entrusted to one person, each domain in turn setting up as many task forces as necessary to cover the questions to be studied;
- The operation to be steered by a committee to be chaired by myself.

Eight domains were identified at Chazay, soon to be completed by a ninth resulting from my search for a solution to take account of the views of the unions and employee representatives (Figure 1.4).

Relations with the unions

I had undertaken to provide the unions with a complete report of the Chazay meeting and to examine with them how to involve the workforce in the process. This exchange of information and negotiation generated several interesting ideas which again reinforced the ownership and above all enabled the unions to play the role of 'objective allies' during the delicate months of January to March 1994, while at the same time remaining officially critical:

- A 'social domain' group completed the plan of action decided at Chazay, with the concern that the social aspects of the change should be taken into account.
- An observer seat was given to the union representatives (excluding the CGT which refused) in each domain group, with the right to alert me if needed, with the final decision in any dispute resting with me and with no appeal.
- A seat was offered to voluntary members of the workforce for each of the task forces created by the domain groups, allowing those at a low organizational level, usually forgotten in this type of situation, to take part in the thinking and the development of solutions.

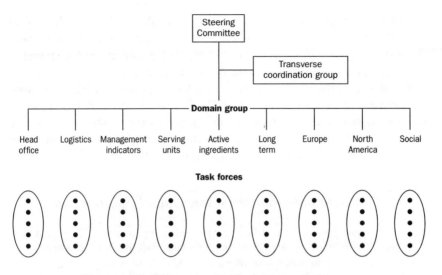

Figure 1.4 Organization chart for steering the SDM project

This plan of action encouraged many relevant remarks and suggestions that were included in the final decisions. The 'social domain' group in particular produced some remarkable work, insisting on the necessary 'equality of worth between the social aspects and the economic aspects of the decisions to be taken'. At the end of the day, even though the unions continued to criticize certain aspects of the approach and voted as a majority against at the central committee of the company which endorsed the project, I gained from them some objective support which allowed some rapid decisions to be taken without being caught up in a very French blocking procedure.

Acceptation of the principle of 'equality of worth between the economic and social' was a deciding factor in the opening of a high quality debate with the unions on the future and necessary evolution of our French 'formulation factories'. The outcome was the introduction of innovatory and empowering solutions in the economic and social field, both during the process of change for the Béziers factory and a little later for the Rousset factory (see box overleaf).

In the fertilizer industry, formulation and conditioning are carried out in formulation factories. The development of new techniques, the opening of frontiers and the improvement of transport, and the reduction in the number of players in the industry are factors that drive towards a reduction in the number of sites.

Rhône-Poulenc Agro had not escaped this rule and had in the period 1987–90 closed or restructured several of its formulation sites. In 1993 there remained in France three formulation sites still in operation: Villefranche-sur-Saône, Béziers and Rousset near Aix-en-Provence.

According to the organizational principles adopted by SDM, the central management of formulations to which the factories were previously attached was eliminated, with the factories in each country combining with the country's distribution activity. It was important to benefit from this transfer in order to simplify and adapt the formulation tool to the needs of the moment.

Custom-made industrial and social approaches

Industrial logic pure and simple would have led to the closure of Béziers and Rousset and regrouping at Villefranche-sur-Saône. But the Béziers factory employed nearly one hundred people in an employment area that was suffering more than 21 per cent unemployment; the Rousset factory, which had just celebrated thirty years with a unique and extraordinary team spirit that had enabled the company to build itself up, deserved more than a simple death sentence.

1. Béziers Factory

Rallying around J.- P. Simmler, Director of Human Resources of Rhône-Poulenc Agro at the beginning of operation SDM and organizer of the 'Beaujolais group', some managers proposed to take over the Béziers factory.

A bespoke arrangement was put in place in which each party was called upon to make a contribution:

- Rhône-Poulenc Agro defined the contractual relationship with the future company, accepted a staged payment and assumed responsibility for the social costs involved in the transfer.
- The Béziers workforce accepted the withdrawal of their Rhône-Poulenc contract together with a 10 per cent reduction in salary in return for shares in the new company as 'compensation'.
- The managers who left Rhône-Poulenc invested their severance payments in the project and took on significant debt in order to launch their company.

Thus CMPA was born (the former name of a company in the Group that had disappeared several years before), which after four years had created forty-eight new jobs (thirteen permanent, thirty-five seasonal, equivalent to full time) had repaid Rhône-Poulenc, increased the workforce salaries to their previous level and which is now a key partner for certain formulations of Rhône-Poulenc Agro.

Such a result was not achieved without some harm. This atypical solution was first criticized by those who did not believe in it, then it was envied for the success of those who had put their enthusiasm and energy into it, before attaining virtual unanimous acceptance today.

2. *Rousset Factory*

The situation at Rousset was different. This small factory with about sixty employees manufactured an ageing product. Investment in a new product at the premises would be difficult, despite the goodwill and remarkable commitment of the teams who were closely linked to a local CGT section whose southern pragmatism had little in common with the national stance of this powerful centralized union.

Thanks to the quality of the men and women at the local level and the quality of the social dialogue at the central level, which had been further enhanced through SDM, it was possible to adopt a bold approach so far as communication and transparency were concerned. It was decided to make a substantial new investment in the Villefranche factory, with the creation of thirty new jobs, while at the same time giving two years' notice of the closure of Rousset in order to facilitate a better transition of production and the outplacement of the workforce.

In this case tears were shed, but there were no strikes to hinder or restrain the process. Once again it was shown how people can understand difficult decisions provided the logic behind them is explained along with the social implications (only two people remained unplaced after turning down more than ten internal or external offers).

As for the Villefranche factory, where a number of new investments have been concentrated, it benefits from renewed morale through its contact with clients and distribution units, and has become a key element in the new organization's plan to reconquer the market.

Communication

If there is one factor that anyone in charge of a process of change must watch, it is communication. In the case of SDM, the briefing session had been the tool for launching the project, then each month a 'key moment' for information and discussion on its progress. There is no substitute for direct communication, backed up by informal contact between staff.

However, it is insufficient in itself and must be supplemented by written communication. This meant a report containing the main messages of the briefing, and for SDM the regular publication of a special internal newsletter giving details of important stages and decisions, this last procedure being used traditionally, but often in too isolated a fashion, in most processes of change.

After all, communication is an art that is not restricted to the tools of the debating chamber, however theoretically perfect they may be. Practice and the ability to listen are essential, as the events of the end of October and the beginning of November 1993 demonstrated. The Chazay meeting had shown the way, identifying our short-term objectives, our long-term vision and our attachment to shared values. I had always clearly stated that if SDM did not *a priori* seek to reduce the workforce, there would no doubt be certain consequences on this front that would have to be expected – to which the unions added 'in recognition of the equality of worth between the economic and the social'.

This declaration, together with the fact that the head office had to be reduced from four hundred to fifty persons, had caused considerable anxiety, especially among the administrative employees. This uncertainty could turn into rejection and I was resolved to remedy this by organizing direct information sessions with the whole of the head office staff.

Over three days, I filled the company meeting room five times; that is, more than five hundred people to whom I described my views and my project, explaining, replying to numerous questions that were often full of good sense, being reassuring when it was possible. In particular, I undertook, in front of these persons who are seldom considered in the company, to return to explain to them what would have been done by the end of the process, that is, in April/May.

In fact I held five meetings in April in the course of which I had particularly to talk about the 'Missions' cell set up to manage those persons temporarily without a job. There were numerous assignment and responsibility changes, but only thirty-nine job losses resulting directly from SDM were announced in March 1994.

To be effective, communication must be tailor-made; it must respond to what people want to know. Furthermore, any unusual procedure, as was the case with the direct sessions with the entire staff, creates an event and strengthens the feeling that something exceptional is happening. That was my objective and it was achieved.

3 Construction

The working groups

The working groups were set up at the end of December and became operational at the beginning of January 1994. In order to be productive within a short period of time, they had adopted the idea of holding two to three day seminar-type meetings, rather than a succession of short meetings organized in 'hidden' time. This was a good choice that enabled conclusions to be reached for certain domains from the beginning of February, the time set for the first meeting of the steering committee.

The framework and orientation provided after the Chazay meeting were sufficiently robust to indicate to each work group the direction in which it should operate. But each had considerable room for manoeuvre, especially in the definition of tools and methods of work.

Two domains were particularly exemplary from the creative viewpoint and they put their mark on the subsequent operations.

The 'management indicators' domain had to look into the appropriate management indicators for a decentralized world. Personally, I had no preconceived ideas on the subject. Guillaume Prache, the young Chief Financial Officer of Rhône-Poulenc Agro and a keen reader of the specialist press, had discovered EVA[3] (Economic Value Added). He was attracted by this approach and had no difficulty in convincing his colleagues of its importance.

A simplified version was developed which was easier to follow and to implement. It became the EVC (Economic Value Created). This new indicator quickly revealed its potential of motivation and relevance for a decentralized organization through allowing those responsible for autonomous units to optimize their decision-making without recourse to judgements other than their own assessments of each situation. It was adopted unit by unit throughout all countries and sometimes even at the level of some factories operating as profit centres, largely due to the commitment and rigour of its 'godfather', Guillaume Prache, who fully assisted me in its introduction (Figure 1.5).

In 1995, we received a visit from the French representative of Stern Stewart who was aiming to promote the concept of EVA. He was astounded by our simplified EVA and told us that to his knowledge we were at the time the only French company using the concept as a management objective.

Two years later, on the initiative of J.-R. Fourtou, EVC was adopted by the entire Rhône-Poulenc Group.

The 'role of head office' domain also showed significant creativity on a difficult subject, that of vision, values and principles of management. From

---

EVC = Operational results + Contributions – Taxes – Cost of employed capital

Operational results	=	Results after amortization, before financial cost and taxes
Contributions	=	Contributions of non-consolidated subsidiaries
Taxes	=	Standard rate of 33 per cent
Capital employed	=	Book value of capital employed (fixed and circulating assets)
Cost of CE	=	CE × 9 per cent, sole weighted rate

EVC = (Results + Contributions) × 0.67 – (Capital employed × 9%)

Figure 1.5 *Calculation formula for EVC*

the outset I had insisted on the importance of vision and values to act as a strongly coherent counterbalance to the decentralized units, because I was convinced of the importance of a 'sense' understood and shared between the different players of the system. It remained for a means to be found for introducing these values and principles into the daily lives of one and all.

The 'role of head office' working group went first for the simplicity option. It decided not to reinvent a charter of values peculiar to Rhône-Poulenc Agro, but rather to rely on the 'principles for action' of the Rhône-Poulenc Group which already existed like many systems of the same type, that is in a document buried in people's drawers which no-one bothered about (see box below).

'Principles for Action' – Vision and Values at the Rhône-Poulenc Group

Our vision

- To be a community of men and women proud of their company on the professional and human level who find personal development in their work as proportional to their commitment.
- To create a leading world group in the life sciences and chemistry and figure among the best in each of our businesses.
- To provide, through our innovations, products and services destined to improve the well-being of people.
- To furnish our customers with answers appropriate to their needs and to develop a partnership with them.
- To secure fidelity from our shareholders and their contribution to the development of the Group, by providing them with a satisfactory return on their investments.

Our values

- *Respect for individuals.* In all our·actions and behaviour we must respect people, their diversity and the cultures of their countries.
- *Safety and environment.* Each one of us must regard as an imperative the safety of persons, equipment, products and the protection of the environment.
- *Integrity.* Over and above each country's legislation, each individual must respect the ethics of his/her profession and act honestly and rigorously.
- *Performance requirement.* Individual and collective performance is a condition of our permanence and of our development. We all have the duty to contribute through our professionalism and commitment.
- *Team spirit.* Team spirit and solidarity are essential for our effectiveness.

Our management principles

- *Give priority to the customer.* Our customers are our raison d'être. We must constantly listen to them, anticipate their needs, and provide them with total quality responses.
- *Facilitate individual development.* Each manager must aim to facilitate development of the competences of his or her colleagues and their career progression. He/she must establish a climate of trust and reciprocal candour and encourage expression and dialogue.
- *Cultivate specificity.* Each entity and every manager must improve the practice of his/her profession and adopt the most effective organization for his/her domain of activity.
- *Safeguard the Group's interests.* Each person, in every decision and action, must take into account not only the interests of his/her own field of activity, but also the more general interests of the Group.
- *Stimulate entrepreneurship.* The organization and management style must, at every level, facilitate individual and collective initiatives and encourage innovation in all areas.
- *Apply the principle of empowerment.* Whatever can be perfectly well carried out at a given level must not be taken over by a higher level. Everyone must be assured that each of his/her colleagues has the necessary means for his/her mission.
- *Be personally committed.* All consultation prior to decision must be genuine. Everyone, in all his/her deeds, is personally committed and assumes responsibility for his/her decisions. He/she watches over the information flowing to and from the people involved.

In order to reanimate this document, the working group envisaged constructing a management questionnaire, based on a set of questions oriented towards the seven management principles of the Group.

Each contributor completes the questionnaire in an anonymous and confidential manner, focusing on the behaviour of his/her manager. After an external analysis the manager receives the results that apply to him or her, corresponding to the set of replies from his/her colleagues (see Figure 1.6). Managers now have a picture of what their colleagues think about their management style and behaviour as compared with the management principles. They must then call a meeting with their team in order to discuss with them and define directions for improvement. Although first conceived of as a voluntary activity, the plan quickly became obligatory for every team of more than five. Some discovered very interesting things about themselves, witness this manager at an enquiry on the questionnaire: 'Very good, well balanced, does badly where he must do badly'; 'Very good tell-tale'.

The seven principles of management

1. Give priority to the customer
2. Facilitate individual development
3. Cultivate specificity
4. Safeguard the Group's interests

5. Stimulate entrepreneurship
6. Apply the principles of empowerment
7. Be personally committed

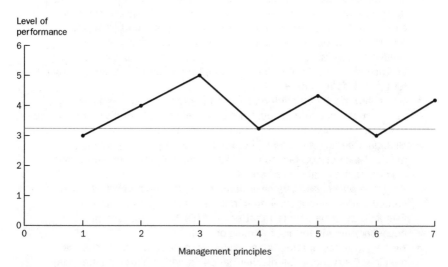

Figure 1.6 *Example of the behaviour profile from the management questionnaire*

This is how the values and principles for action, transmitted through communication and strong commitment by the managers, came to be part of everyday life. Even today, it is not rare to find people in the company who react by quoting these values, such as in reference to situations, events or behaviours that they judge to be incompatible with them. In my opinion this is a sign of the good health of the company and its staff.

The 'role of the head office' working group also proposed the identification of the rights and duties of decentralized entrepreneurs. This provoked publication under the name 'yellow lines' of a list of simple and concrete rules showing everyone how to behave in certain precisely defined situations.

The 'Yellow Lines', Agro Sector, June 1995

- The objective of Agro is maximum decentralization of responsibility.
- Each unit takes the values and principles of the sector as its own and communicates and applies them.
- Outside the centre, in the bounds of their domains of responsibility, functional managers may not give instructions directly to operational staff.
- The recruitment, development, and departure of persons reporting directly to the director of a decentralized unit require the backing of a supervisor.
- Business units are forbidden to purchase a 'core' active ingredient from outside.
- If a commercial unit declines to develop an active ingredient, the 'Active Ingredients' unit may make an offer to a competitor in this country. The terms may not be better than internal terms.
- Zones may not determine alone the local risks above a threshold negotiated with the head office for each country.
- Subcontracting: prior consultation is obligatory. Service units, research units and formulation plants have the right of first refusal on any study or project that might be placed externally. They will be informed of the final contract. The results may be audited.
- A unit which takes a decision that impacts on another unit must inform that unit in advance. Although recourse to arbitration always remains possible, in practice it must be seen as a last resort.

A position of operational auditor was created close to the chief executive officer to ensure that the new organization functioned well in respect of these values and principles. By replacing the traditional methods of control, it indicated clearly that the confidence placed in everyone had its counterpart: that confidence had to be deserved. One could quote many other examples of the creativity of working parties during this period.

The amount of energy put in was considerable and it enabled the operation to be managed in an extremely short period of time:

- start of working groups: 3 January 1994;
- first proposals to steering committee: 31 January 1994;
- final proposals to steering committee: 14 and 15 March 1994.

This work had been accompanied by five meetings of the company central committee, involving unions, to ratify the intermediary decisions and then the final proposals on 31 March 1994. On this date, the steering committee and the working groups were dissolved and the final managers were appointed. They took charge of the process for implementing the agreed organizations. It took several months for these new organizations to settle down, leaving many people temporarily without a position and requiring them to call upon the help of the 'Missions' cell that had been created especially to manage these particularly unpleasant situations of transition.

Protecting the project

For three months, during the course of which the detail of the organization and its tools were developed, I was certainly under considerable strain, but I was not involved in the acts of construction, apart from the steering committees and the central committee meetings. I spent most of my time supervising the mobilization of volunteers and protecting the project.

I needed to strengthen myself in the face of doubts that might arise here or there. On several occasions I had several informal meetings with consultant friends to seek their opinions and their encouragement. Jean-René Fourtou had also asked me to keep him informed and had offered to make himself available when necessary, 'not as chairman, but as consultant', he stressed – a separation of roles that appears none too clear, but which worked effectively in the majority of cases.

I met him four times at my request during the process and he definitely played a major role in speeding up decision implementation. His words of 'advice' obviously carried more weight than those of an ordinary consultant, and I fanned the flames – with his support – a little beyond my own convictions in order to go fast, faster and still faster, in particular when it came to appointing the future managers and having them take over after the 'domain' groups. In retrospect I must admit that he was right, for because of this, the project did not have time to run out of steam as it might have done.

I also appealed to Jean-René Fourtou and other members of the executive committee of Rhône-Poulenc who supported my approach to guarantee the protection of the project. The atypical approach that I was using was challenged by some directors within the Group, and it only took one meeting of the champions of the traditional method for rumours to reach me that nobody in the Group believed in what I was doing.

Depending on the source of these rumours, at times I felt wounded, even destabilized. Hence my recourse to the support of powerful and well-placed allies. With the passage of time and the feeling that I had of being on the right path, I became less sensitive to these criticisms and when in March I again received thoughts on my approach, I made it clear that I would not compromise. I staked my position and my mission in order to obtain the autonomy and calmness of spirit necessary to continue. But having done this in writing at the end of the week, I spent the weekend with my wife wondering if I would still have my job on the Monday morning. I would in fact have left if I had not been able to carry out the operation in the way that I envisaged it.

The choice of people

The project was developed with the people already in place and a real human adventure took shape during the adoption phase and then in the construction phase.

The theories about the resistance to the phenomena of change – technical, political and cultural, which I discovered from reading several books, militated in favour of a renewal of staff. The first internal reactions to the announcement of SDM also indicated that I would not be able to build a decentralized organization with people who had shown centralizing skills. I decided however to 'go with', giving more weight to human 'glue' and team spirit than to the import of outside elements ostensibly better suited to the situation, but more difficult to integrate. I must admit that at heart I have always felt an intuitive mistrust of 'providential persons', even though I have seen some who were remarkably successful.

My own team remained the same throughout the period of implementing the change. Only a few lower level managers did not find a place in the new organization, generally because of the gap between what they thought they could do and what they were offered. In such cases, they left the Group with a comfortable severance and my support to help them in their new career. After all, perhaps they were right to believe in a hidden potential that the company had not been able to uncover.

The real changes in personnel took place during 1995 as a result of opportunities created by voluntary departures, or because the results or performance were not as expected. My most serious problem concerned the American management team which, as I had suspected for several months but had decided to live with, did not accept the planned division for the different activities carried out in the US (research, production, distribution). Prudence is necessary when as director of a French company one wishes to further the careers of American managers. This is why I took my time and acted gently, after preparing a British manager who had closely followed the SDM operation to take over subsequently. The British are well able to bridge the two cultures and being generally courageous, mobile and competitive are a breeding ground of expertise favoured for international development. This was a good decision which, doubtless for the first time, brought on board an American team totally in tune with the rest of the organization and ready to participate in innovation and growth.

Apart from this episode, I had decided to keep the same staff. Was it the best solution? Definitely yes, because I felt very well with this team and because, when it comes to human relations, it seems to me to be the predominant element. But I would certainly beware of making it a universal rule, for in the world of people and the judgements that one makes about them it behoves one to be modest.

Nevertheless, we had clearly stated in the SDM operation rules that the sanctions system – positive or negative – would be stronger than in the past. Witness the unusual variable remuneration systems that were developed along with the improvement of the EVC. In another sense, difficult decisions led me a little later into dispute with some general managers of units concerning inadequate results. This new business practice, which was sometimes challenged, had the effect of turning them from the status of system barons into that of committed entrepreneurs, after I had once again explained the rules of the game and the reasons for my decisions.

4 Launch and Follow-up

I had fixed an international conference on 1, 2 and 3 June 1994 in order to clarify with all 'entrepreneurs' the new company methods of operation. All the newly appointed top executives were there, but in contrast to the October 1993 meeting at Chazay I had invited several new participants, the managing directors of small units (FF20 to 30 m annual turnover), as I wished to show that they too formed a cornerstone of the system. I gave the closing address that I had carefully prepared and which was taken to be the true launch of the new organization.

After reviewing the achievements of the past months, which helped to create the necessary emotional charge for the grand departure, I again stated what I expected from SDM.

'We have provided ourselves with a new organization based on a clear principle: get close to our clients. What we have tried to build is an organization in which the roles have been well and clearly defined, with a much-reduced central administration and 'business units' that are closer to their clients. Between these two lie the units of raw materials production, research and services, which operate in relation to clients/suppliers on the basis of real needs from one to the other. By this approach we expect to eliminate everything that is not useful to the main priority, what one working group called 'stupid work'.

'We have provided ourselves with a number of new tools to make our new organization function better and in a more responsive manner:
- A new pertinent cost system that offers permanent pertinent information on costs to commercial managers and therefore facilitates a much faster response;
- A complete economic indicator provided by the EVC for the manager;
- A comparison in relation to year N–1 rather than in relation to a theoretical budget which, in a period of uncertainty, does not say much;
- A simplification of the budget processes to allow more time to the commercial staff and their clients;
- The possibility of external subcontracting if the internal suppliers do not maintain their competitive edge (it is for them to adapt to remain in the running);
- The introduction of variable remuneration systems linked to the specific results of each business.

'However, an organization and its tools are not enough if there is no change in our behaviour. It is for us to put these changes to work to achieve our objectives which I shall state once again:
- In the short term, to improve our results rapidly: FF200 m in 1994, FF500 m in 1995 compared with 1993.
- In the long term, at the horizon of 2000 to remain in the world leaders

group of the profession. To have placed FF4 bn worth of new products on the market during the year 2000.

– In the long term, to have redefined the manner in which our research is organized to find the products for 2010 that will probably be used at the rate of a few grammes per hectare. This redefinition will require a complete recasting of our approach and our tools, new food for thought for ourselves and our researchers.

'All the above is governed by our ability to achieve growth, add to our market share and thereby improve our results. For I would remind you again that even though we must be vigilant on costs, our strategy is not based *a priori* on a reduction of fixed costs. With this in mind, our action must revolve around four axes, which may appear contradictory, but it is for each person to find the right balance between them in his unit and in his company. These axes are:

1. Dynamism and entrepreneurial spirit;
2. Capacity for innovation everywhere;
3. Professionalism and quality;
4. Competitive costing and pricing.

All to be done while observing the values and principles for action that I ask you to carry high.'

Thus SDM took off, boosted by hundreds of players wanting the operation to succeed because they had had a hand in writing it.

The period of following-up SDM after its launch lasted for me from the end of 1994 to the end of 1996, when I ceased to be Chief Executive Officer of Rhône-Poulenc Agro. It was definitely – along with my service in Portugal (see Part 2) – one of the richest periods of my professional life.

My personal workload had decreased appreciably, as measured by my daily mail which had dropped by 90 per cent. Month after month, the financial results improved; I had no more worries on that score. This state of affairs left me the time and the freedom of spirit to engage personally in the follow-up process and to discover a fresh role, that of resource provider. The working groups of the launch conference of June 1994 had identified the approach to clients and networking as topics that required to be worked on in particular. To give effect to this, I took on a young manager and an external consultant, who launched and directed a number of pilot schemes with the units. I could, through them, take the temperature of what was going on in the teams and I was sure that, thanks to this support, actions on the ground would really be implemented. This work allowed concrete progress to be made and contributed to the awareness and training of several groups, in particular those in less structured small countries that had greater need of support than others.

These topics were regularly reworked on the theme 'Enriching SDM' during international conferences at the end of 1994 and the beginning of 1995, while the 1996 conference was especially oriented towards networking.

These meetings, to which I devoted much effort, greatly helped the process to become enhanced and strengthened and to advance. There were also – and are still – convivial occasions for all participants, boosted every two years by the award of 'Golden Orchids', a non-financial acknowledgement of the most deserving teams in Agro.

The second level of follow-up developed on the ground, where I at last had the time to go back and talk with the local teams, understand them, encourage them and help them to appreciate better the global meaning of their local actions. I visited the US in particular, where adjustments to the organization and staffing were necessary, and Asia, where an ambitious setting-up strategy had been launched.

It was during one of these visits to Thailand in April 1995 that I had the occasion to verify for the first time the value of the new approach to objectives that we had developed to take account of the uncertainties in which our markets were evolving. This approach was based on three levels:

- *Commitments:* what people are engaged in doing;
- *Hopes:* what they can hope for/envisage on the basis of the concrete evidence concerning the product and its markets;
- *Dreams:* what might happen if what at present seems unlikely became a fact.

We were planning to build a factory for our new insecticide Fipronil that was especially suitable for the rice-growing market and would subsequently become a huge commercial success. It is precisely because the teams in the Asian zone appeared to me to believe in their *hopes* that I returned to France convinced that we should accelerate the start of construction work on the factory.

The decision was taken by rushing through the procedures – an investment of FF500 m was involved – and the project was entrusted to an interdisciplinary team that by juggling between the costs of speed and safety made it possible for the first tons of Fipronil to emerge from the Elbeuf factory in the spring of 1997, eight months before the originally planned date. We were then short of product following development of the markets between hopes and dreams. The empowerment of the teams had been responsible for this remarkable success which for the company represented several hundred million FF of results.

The third level of follow-up was the defining and implementation of a huge programme of training in 'entrepreneurship' that involved more than three hundred international managers and was carried out through thirteen residential seminars spread over three years. This serious training, which had a budget of more than FF10m, rounded off the change in thought process and behaviour that had been initiated with SDM. In fact, it fitted in with a broader programme that Jean-René Fourtou wanted for the whole of the Group.

As it was, the adaptation work that I undertook with the directors and professors of CEDEP led to the establishment of a module specifically suited to the particular case of Agro. It was at this point that Daniel Muzyka, professor at INSEAD and at CEDEP, became interested in the SDM experience and suggested that he produce a business case study on it. He wrote the case study using all the documents that I had kept and from numerous recorded interviews in France, the United States and Britain.

Claude Michaud, director of CEDEP, was also interested in the SDM case and embarked on research into the styles of management that came from the experience, research that continues today with his colleague, Jean-Claude Thoenig.

For those who attended those seminars, beginning with myself, it was a striking revelation to discover the theoretical foundations of the implementation of autonomy that had often been achieved quite intuitively in the SDM experience.

The contributions from Professor Degan Morris on management indicators and the concept of pertinent cost completely validated the choices made by showing them in a new and reassuring light.

Pertinent cost defines the manufacturing cost of a product in a factory that has a production rate close to its theoretical maximum capacity (90 per cent).

Pertinent cost is therefore the opposite of computed cost which, taking into account the effects of possible under-production, sometimes leads to results that are incompatible with market realities (Figure 1.7).

When supported by an appropriate marketing policy, pertinent cost, in contrast to computed cost, allows a virtuous circle to be set in motion ensuring redeployment and coming out on top.

The importance of the shared vision and individual commitment in effective teams was also recalled through cases and lively discussions. Both

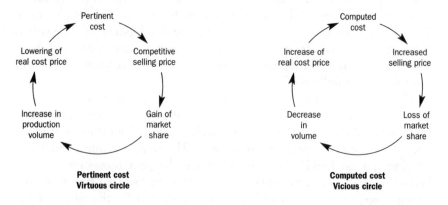

Figure 1.7 *Pertinent cost*

functional and operational managers from different countries met on this occasion and this marked the start of informal networks.

I had undertaken to come and spend a half-day with each group to remind them of the vision, meaning and principles that lay behind SDM. My address was followed by a lively question and answer session covering all topics, and then by additional individual discussions at subsequent meals.

When at the end of 1996 I ceased to be chief executive officer of Rhône-Poulenc Agro, I strongly recommended my successor to adopt the same approach for the remaining two seminars. This he did to the great satisfaction of himself and the participants.

This transverse training played an important part in the change begun by SDM, by strengthening the players' understanding of what had happened and through exercises that made them more aware of the type of entrepreneurial behaviour that we wished to promote. In this sense, it allowed everyone to sign up for the duration, thus facilitating the adjustments to come.

5 Epilogue

In December 1996, a few weeks before taking up my new position and joining the executive committee of Rhône-Poulenc, I was to hold my last 'flash info' briefing. I knew that at this last meeting I would have to control a strong emotional charge and I wondered how I would be able to offer thanks and good wishes to these men and women who had accompanied me in the adventure.

Then I received from Vincent Lenhardt a copy of his book *Oser la Confiance*, written with Bertrand Martin and Bruno Jarrosson. Looking quickly through it, the epilogue by Bertrand Martin on his experience caught my eye. I read it closely and was taken with its form and substance. It expressed precisely what I wanted to say about what I had experienced throughout these last three years.

I do not like to read out speeches written by others, but on this occasion I decided to read out this very fine text at the end of my final briefing. Here it is.

> This story, like all stories, may give rise to many readings because of the fact that reality blends people and events in such an inextricable and complex fashion that is incapable of any synthetic reduction.
>
> Product quality, people's ability and labour, shareholder perseverance, jumping at danger, finally smiling at fortune, all this is true. And success is never acquired. That may be so, but it is also true that for years an exceptional collective commitment persisted and developed, allowing challenges to be accepted, rationally viewed unachievable targets to be attained and breakdowns at key moments to be avoided.
>
> The energy that I had so often seen used in destructive internal battles was this time used positively, the vital energy of men and women players responsible for their destiny, all together. This resulted not from a new miracle formula, but from profound changes in attitude and behaviour, never given for granted, always questioned, proof of truth before others and oneself.
>
> Rational, certain, mechanical, organized and controlled functioning had given way to the logic of the living, the desire to act, enthusiasm, passion but also that of the unexpected, the chaotic, doubt, questioning, fear.
>
> Can one unite the energy of the irrational with the solidity of the rational?
>
> Is it sensible to tell the complete truth in order to stimulate reaction and commitment? For it is not always nice to speak the full truth. But isn't a truncated truth, however slight, the beginning of a manipulation? Lying is not far behind and that destroys commitment for a long time.
>
> Isn't this trust which is born and nurtured through reciprocity an illusion? And yet this is how the one builds from the other. And distrust, however minimal, is destructive.
>
> Permitting adoption that stimulates motivation is allowing oneself to be deprived of rights. Is it acceptable, is it even normal for the person who has the

responsibility of power to abandon it in this way, to abandon the exercising of power, even partially? Power is so enjoyable.

Respecting the words and thoughts of other persons, allowing them their freedom of space to exercise their talents and responsibility, to develop their judgement, is very difficult when one believes that one is guardian of the truth. It is very comforting to believe that one knows it. The head of a company said to me: 'The most difficult thing for me is to keep quiet when I know the solution.'

Giving autonomy, the freedom to allow the person to grow, doesn't it run the risk of errors, accidents and confusion? Breaking a regime that is frozen, that prevents advancement, to allow a chaotic disorder to become established from which life will spring, is that really acceptable?

Unlike technical problems that are amenable to solutions, these questions are interrogations that are never concluded, like appeals, ever open windows to a better future. The answers lie within each of us. They depend on what we are, on what we think about ourselves and others, our vision of society and the world, our internal strengths and convictions, but also our limitations and our fears.

Attempting to respond is accepting to call ourselves into question again and advancing is an individual and collective expedition in which each confident step, each stage reached, is a new point of departure.

These were our questions and thoughts from the day after the big bang that was our company meeting. I wanted to testify our own advancement in order to pay due homage to all the participants and players, but also to make a modest contribution to an evolution that appears to me to be both desirable and inescapable.

The stakes are considerable for the company, for individuals, and for the whole of society. If this testimony encourages people to put their faith in trust, then these words will have achieved their aim.

The twentieth century will have seen the triumph of the rational and of mechanized work, the twenty-first will perhaps see the triumph of the humanized company. That would be good news.

Extract from *Oser la Confiance*,
B. Martin, V. Lenhardt and B. Jarrosson, 1996.[4]

I had this typed up and distributed to all, adding the following handwritten note: 'I endorse these remarks as my own as they reflect my own convictions about management. My thanks to all for your confidence. Continue the good work. A fair wind to Agro!' This was my goodbye, or rather my *au revoir* gift to this formidable team.

Four years later, the environment had changed, with the arrival of plant biotechnologies that in the longer term will transform the agrochemical profession and present new challenges. The Rhône-Poulenc Group has changed profoundly, confirming definitively its swing towards the life sciences, human, plant and animal health.

Rhône-Poulenc Agro, attached to the holding company Rhône-Poulenc Plant and Animal Health, has substantially altered its legal structure. A new chief executive officer took over from me at the head of Rhône-Poulenc Agro. Though I remain supervisor, I make it a point of honour to allow him to operate in his own way in a framework that I nevertheless defined precisely in a written note that describes my vision of the organization: 'based on the pursuit of the best balance between the two principles that might at first appear in opposition to one another:

 – *Autonomy* given to entrepreneurs in order to take decisions as close as possible to clients and to the ground with the minimum of constraints (what Anglo-Saxons understand as freedom to act);
 – *Accepted constraints*, represented by the commitment to respect the values and principles for action of the Group.

Achieving a balance between these two ideas – true decentralization in a true Group – requires permanent vigilance on the part of managers with regard to their own behaviour and the decisions that they take in the sight of all. The regulatory role of the chief executive officer is of course fundamental.'

Four years on, the enthusiasm of managers to enhance EVC remains, as it becomes rooted in a new culture. Also when, as is obviously necessary in a living company, modifications, adjustments or the introducing of new working processes are put in hand, this is always done after due forethought to establish that they conform to the 'SDM spirit', which has put its stamp on those who lived through this adventure and who wish to pursue it in the same vein.

Alain Godard
August 1998

Notes

1 *Oser la Confiance*, op. cit.
2 By 'centre', I mean here and in the remainder of the book the group of people outside direct hierarchies who, by their functions or the use that they make of them, assume that they have the 'sovereign' right to intervene in the functioning and the priorities of decentralized units.
3 Registered trademark of a concept developed by Stern Stewart.
4 *Oser la Confiance*, op. cit.

PART 2

Lessons from an Experience

Alain Godard interviewed by Vincent Lenhardt

Alain Godard wrote the first part as a chronological narrative. It seemed useful to us to extract the lessons from this experience. Certain stages and certain facts appeared significant. We wished to underline these together in this second part.

In other respects, implementation of such an operation requires focusing on certain major stakes and their handling presupposes strong convictions. Alain Godard would not have been able to carry SDM through without having made choices, not only of management priorities but also of values based on his convictions. It seemed to us essential to highlight these.

Finally, such an operation demands from its person in command a set of professional and personal qualities that require a whole course of preparation and experience. We chose to take the time to go over it together.

Vincent Lenhardt

1 Review of Events

Figure 1.1 (page 4) identifies two periods where the results increased: 1987–90 corresponding to the acquisition of Union Carbide and 1994–96 corresponding to SDM. Can one describe both as periods of 'refounding'?

I think so, to the extent that these two periods were generators of an extraordinary internal energy. A major acquisition such as Union Carbide creates an obligation for change and for results that galvanize the will. On this score, Philippe Desmarescaux who was chairman and chief executive officer of Rhône-Poulenc Agro knew remarkably well how to make us give of our best.

In the case of SDM, the stakes at the beginning were to convince people in the company that a major change – as important as that associated with an acquisition – was necessary to bring us out of the crisis.

Nevertheless, the levers of improvement in results are fundamentally different in the case of a 'refounding' brought about by an external obligation – a merger linked to an acquisition – and that arising from an internal obligation – extricating a company from a crisis. The term 'refounding' does remain valid in both cases, because we are ultimately concerned with organizations and functions that are totally new in comparison with the pre-established systems at the start.

The graph uses the concept of operational results, whereas in your SDM experience the EVC became the reference indicator. What significance did this indicator have in the success of SDM?

A much greater significance than I imagined. Being neither a theoretician nor a designer, I had not thoroughly considered the importance of management indicators in the players' change of behaviour.

But it is obvious that if you give autonomy to the manager of a profit centre judging him on the operational results – that is, without taking into account the amount of capital employed in this profit centre – he will implicitly go for the generation of pure margin and not watch closely enough the level of capital employed. To put it clearly, a tradesman, to be sure of not losing sales, will tend to build up his stock or allow his clients accounts to spin out.

EVC, which makes him pay for his capital employed (at a 9 per cent rate in the Rhône-Poulenc model) naturally reminds him to look for the right balance. The great advantage of EVC for management has been to move from a complex system where head office required calculations on each line of the operating account to a simple system where managers were only accountable for the final figure. It was up to them to define the best combination between volumes, prices, fixed costs, working capital, and so on. All observers of the SDM experience, internal and external, have noted the federative role of EVC and how it brought coherence and motivation with it.

I should also like to say a word about another change made in the management system which had an important impact on behaviour. This was the move from a *standard cost*, calculated as a function of the estimated production volumes, to a cost that we described as *commercial cost* (or *pertinent cost*) based on the theoretical capacity of the production plant. I had discovered this concept in Tom Peters' work, and it had subsequently been clarified by Professor Degan Morris at the CEDEP leadership training sessions. *Pertinent cost*, which is separate from the volumes actually produced, is the only cost that gives the isolated salesperson the possibility of reacting quickly using the only pertinent information, namely that corresponding to the *real* cost price of the sold product if the factory that produces it operates at full capacity, which largely depends on commercial success.

The beneficial effect of this approach is immediate. In addition, it greatly simplifies budget-making by avoiding the permanent comings and goings between the commercial services and production departments which spend ages producing figures that have no meaning, only to finish up with 'standard costs' that are both false and not pertinent.

Out of all this I have learnt an important lesson about the generally underestimated effect of management indicators on the behaviour of managers.

You give an indicator for safety. What meaning does it have for you?

Safety is a key value for a Group like Rhône-Poulenc that makes use of sophisticated production technologies. But safety is also part of behaviour in the simplest daily acts.

What is interesting to me in the figures for the Group and for Rhône-Poulenc Agro is that one can see astonishing improvements in the results from the moment that measurement and motivation begin. The ways to improvement and the new tools emerge from the attention that people pay them, and again the virtuous cycle is established. During the crisis years, all players in the company were mobilized on safety and they made it an object of pride, which in a certain sense compensates in people's heads for the devastating effects of a collapse in the financial results.

Personally, I was not particularly prepared to conduct a safety campaign, but I quickly came to appreciate that to begin every meeting with the safety record, as our more formalistic American friends did, was not merely a gimmick. The example set by the top executive can lead to real changes in behaviour.

The day my colleagues and their teams began to understand that my commitment to safety was as great as my commitment to the financial results they set to work to relay the message and change people's behaviour. For me it is proof that an organization can mobilize itself from top to bottom on concepts that are not *a priori* evident to everyone. First of all, as always, it is a question of the sincerity, transparency and example of senior management.

What was produced for safety, one value among many, should extend to the other values and principles of the organization. It is therefore an encouraging pointer for the future.

Maturing

The summer of 1993 is for you a key period of coming to maturity. How did the different internal and external factors become mutually enriched to convince you that a way out was possible?

The point of departure is no doubt quite personal. I do not like to lose and I am generally convinced that there is always a solution to a difficulty. I also hate not having control of the events that I am in principle managing. 'Don't surrender' is a phrase that often comes to mind when there is a difficulty; it forces one to be creative in finding solutions.

In the case of the crisis that struck Rhône-Poulenc Agro, the situation was very complex to analyse. It was incontestably my reading of Tom Peters that helped me to become aware of solutions, thanks to the numerous examples he analyses and the iconoclastic tone that truly incites one to revolution. I remember that as I read him, I saw the company that I was in charge of reflecting its defects and unwieldiness as in a magnifying mirror. The attachment that I had developed for these recommendations was probably exaggerated, almost mystical. I had to save Agro and I was ready to set off on crusade.

The fact that Jean-René Fourtou is a fervent supporter of the concept of decentralization probably played a reassuring role so far as the method envisaged was concerned. Tom Peters's recipes which I had made my own were not completely foolish because they led in a direction supported by the Group chairman. This is my *a posteriori* analysis, but at the time, I was unaware of it, being swept along by the conviction that I had at last found a solution.

I recognize today that such a course of events, that had led me to accumulate considerable internal energy, might have led to great disappointments if the envisaged solutions had not been the right ones. But I imagine that if that had been the case, the chairman would have prevented me from implementing them.

Is it easy to have one's chairman as consultant?

The role of Jean-René Fourtou is in fact interesting to analyse. His previous experience as a consultant at the highest level – thirty years with Bossard Consultants as chairman founder – is rare for the chairman of a large international industrial Group. It allowed him to develop his own vision of the place of the company and its functioning as a polycellular system.

A few years after his arrival at Rhône-Poulenc, he had been bearer of the formula 'a true decentralization in a true Group' and initiator of thoughts on 'action principles'. But he was waiting for something to start somewhere in order to take advantage of the dynamic thus created and then move his pawn. It is in this sense that my will to launch myself into a policy of decentralization announced as a drastic measure captured his interest and he asked me to come and see him regularly and to keep him informed, and in fact saying: 'I will be your consultant, not your chairman'. This was true for the majority of our exchanges, except for one occasion when, more chairman than consultant, he showed a certain unease which I attributed to rumours that were circulating about my methods. This unsettled me somewhat at a time when I needed to feel confidence around me.

Apart from this episode that probably was not important for him (one always underestimates the effect of an unfortunate remark, or one perceived as such, on another person), he gave me valuable support at the psychological and methodological level, encouraging me and backing me whenever necessary. He influenced me especially in regard to everything that touched upon the speed of implementation: announcement of decisions, appointment of new managers, and so on.

After the start up of the new organization, he was its most ardent defender in public, quoting it as an example and summarizing it perfectly as two points: utilization of EVC and putting 'action principles' into practice. His aim was to draw the rest of the Group along in a movement, not an identical one, but one inspired by the same principles. This was how EVC became the priority indicator used by all managers of the Group, even if its method of application varies according to sector.

Why did you decide to do without a consultant?

People like myself, who have long been operators on the ground, have little time to reflect. In this sense the contribution of consultants who observe, analyse and select processes or methods is indispensable. But in my opinion, except in special circumstances, the consultant should take care to remain in his role of support, while of course complementing this with training which belongs to his privileged domain.

Too often in my career I have seen consultants called in by management boards who, without any real participative procedure, have rolled out a method more or less suitable for the situation, and then actually taken the place of the managers in order to make it work at a faster rate. There is often a certain efficiency about the whole, but one cannot expect the employees to feel fundamentally party to such an approach. In reality, they implement it under constraint and pressure, or take the easy route of conspiring with the consultant to find indicators or ratios that demonstrate the efficiency of the mission.

In the SDM experience, I sought approval and mobilization which seemed to me to be essential preliminaries for the success of the operation. The company had come from two reorganizations in which consultants had been quite heavily involved; a third restructuring organized in the same manner would have been put in the same category as the first two and would not have been experienced as a cultural shock or as a refounding, however necessary.

Furthermore, I had at hand all the elements that the top executive generally seeks from the consultant. On the one hand, I had accumulated sufficient internal energy to launch the operation and therefore had no need of the 'auxiliary generating unit', that constitutes the consultant, in order to get the executive started. On the other hand, thanks to the experience of the Union Carbide merger, I had an 'up and running' method, and a number of colleagues who had put it into practice. At this point the risk of failure seemed slight.

In a rather amusing way, during September 1993, I chanced to mention to one of the senior consultants of the firm that was coming to the end of a traditional mission for us, the procedures that I was in the process of carrying out. Surprised by the scale of the project, he predicted an inescapable failure if I did not take on consultants. Even though he had a vested interest, I believe that he was sincere in what he said. But on the one side he underestimated the existing experience, and on the other the energy that can be self-generated from mobilization around a 'chosen' project, together with the rejection that can be produced in the end by too high a dose of consultancy in a company.

This being the case, in order to make myself fully understood on this delicate matter (there will no doubt be readers who are consultants), I should point out that between September 1994 and June 1995 I engaged a well-known consultant to facilitate the introduction of procedures concerning the approach to clients and networking which were considered to be priorities for the further enrichment of SDM. But this contribution was in keeping with a context understood by all as improvement of functioning in points of detail where, it was clear, we lacked knowledge and experience.

How do you analyse your 'bookish' relationship with the highly regarded consultant Tom Peters?

Reading the book by Tom Peters corresponds to this need for reflection and method that I mentioned earlier. Having to face up to the problem in front of me, and finding out by chance about the book *Liberation Management* which seemed to answer my questions, I chose the tool of reading to gain access to them. But I would not have been able to acquire the same thing from a seminar on the subject. For me the book remains, in a more rarely used (and I would add less onerous) form, a contribution of the consultant's skills.

I found in it things that I would not have invented by myself, or would not have implemented without referring to successful experience elsewhere. For example, the principle of pertinent cost, placing internal services in competition with external subcontracting, or the replacement of inefficient or obsolete macro systems with the harmonious combination of pencil, rubber and common sense.

As I have said elsewhere, the tone of the book incited a 'revolutionary' approach that brought oxygen and renewal into a conformist operating style that is sometimes stifling.

Validation and ownership

The thinking group that is working on the 'social barometer' invites you at the end of August 1993. At your meeting with them you use it to test your ideas and round off your thoughts. How do you explain this?

When the results of the 'social barometer' came out at the beginning of 1993 I analysed them and endorsed the creation of the thinking group, undertaking to go and meet them. But I have to confess that the events of that summer and my personal search for a solution caused me to forget this. When I received their invitation to go to meet them in Beaujolais where they had their seminar, my first reaction was to think that I had something else to do. But being a man of my word, I went. It was as I heard them telling me what stage they had reached in their thinking that it became obvious to me that it complemented what was to become SDM. I 'offered' them SDM as a ripe fruit such as it had become in my head. I think it was this unprepared act, which was therefore sincere and received as such, that provoked their supportive reaction, followed by encouragement and advice.

While I am persuaded that this event played an important role in the awareness that something new was about to happen and therefore in the subsequent adoption of the project, I do not see how one could have constructed such a scenario in a voluntary way. Perhaps one can imagine that if this event had not occurred, I had reached such a level of determination and preparation that I would have used some other opportunity.

One of the conclusions that can be drawn from this experience is that one cannot prepare everything, perhaps even that one should not prepare everything, but one should leave room for solutions to emerge that one should be ready to use in order to make progress. Allowing room for intuition and feeling in order to adapt to the circumstances of an increasingly uncertain environment is probably one of the rules for the manager of tomorrow.

By disclosing information to an inter-hierarchical group you ran the risk of marginalizing your own executive board. How did it react?

As I have just explained, my communication to this inter-hierarchical group was not premeditated. But in informing them, I implicitly took the risk of having my executive board call me to account. In fact, I knew my world well enough, and given that the 'social barometer' group had been set up by the board itself, my action was integrated with an approach that was implicitly authorized. On the contrary, the positive response from the 'social barometer' group which I relayed to my board helped to reassure them and to create a *de facto* committed supporter of the SDM project.

This being the case, either as a player or as chairman, I have seen many executive boards in operation that have made me very critical of this type of structure. It is rare for everyone to be attentive at the same time and, statistically, there are always 25 per cent of those present who are thinking of other things or doing their correspondence.

This observation led me (once again supported by Tom Peters) to abolish executive boards in the SDM organization, and to replace them by *ad hoc* committees attended only by the managers leading the project in question, but which their colleagues could without obligation attend if they wished. This system worked well and was in tune with the drive for simplification and the avoidance of unnecessary things.

Too many 'high mass' weekly or monthly meetings whose usefulness is questionable continue to exist in large organizations, and I believe that the time wasted by managers is considerable, giving pause for thought on an area insufficiently explored in relation to the debate on the organization of working time. From experience, I have nevertheless noted the reticence of senior managers to abandon the status conferred by membership of the executive board, and the attempts to have it restored that begin as soon as it is removed.

To avoid having to do this, I established a strategic committee with an important role that would meet three times a year to discuss fundamental topics in a semi-residential context. I found that this solution was much more effective than the traditional executive board meeting monthly, or even more frequently, to discuss more or less interesting problems of the day whose solutions could be found much closer to the ground.

This remains a difficult area of evolution, given the reticence of the players, and one should only opt for such a change if one feels that one has sufficient energy to stay the course. Otherwise, it is better to be pragmatic and to accept a few 'high masses' considered to be essential by the players themselves to maintain their status and recognition, along with their motivation even.

What importance do you attach to communication in its various forms and in the different stages of the process?

There is never enough communication, which is not to say that we do not produce enough transparencies, or nowadays videos or CD ROMs. The wastage from traditional communication systems is incontestable and substantial economies could be made in raw material.

Some internal publications have a significant role for informing and developing the membership spirit that is useful for motivating teams. Others are mainly intended to boost the egos of those who produce them. From experience, I have done away with several on numerous occasions without a single reader noticing. But in large organizations, new publications appear immediately, always with impeccable justification.

For me, true communication is verbal; I would even say physical. This is why from 1992 I set up the briefings, which proved to be remarkable communication tools. So much so that in 1996, when I questioned whether they should continue, internal surveys revealed unanimously that it would be a serious error to abandon them. They are in operation today under my successor.

Using the briefing as an aid for the communication of SDM was therefore the most natural and the most effective method. The challenge was to find a tone and content that created the event. I had the advantage from my own professional experience of having been a salesman 'on the ground' where I had to persuade farmers, people with commonsense, to buy products to protect their fields. Selling is a game that is constantly renewed and quickly intoxicating for anyone who gets involved in it. It is an excellent exercise that every manager should have practised in his or her career because it develops an essential quality for management: listening.

The same goes for communication, which is only good and effective as long as one understands what the other intended. One can then find the tone, the form and the words to turn an ordinary meeting into a success. This is why, so far as I am concerned, I consider it impossible to delegate the preparation of a speech or a presentation. On the rare occasions when I have had to do this, I have always felt uncomfortable and, when all is said, bad.

Of course, written backup is necessary, to complement the verbal. But it should above all be regarded as a tool allowing the hierarchy to flow down the verbal message, something we always insisted upon in relation to the briefings. The other essential element for ensuring good communication is the ability to capture what is said in the company, that is, to listen and make use of what is heard. Throughout the concentrated period of SDM, the communication department of Agro, because it considered itself a participant, played this role marvellously, using all its contacts and all its antennae to take the pulse of the social body. It was they who informed me of the great disquiet among the workforce, which led me to meet the whole of the staff face to face at the beginning and at the end of the operation.

I had shown my willingness to meet everyone, by calling people together in groups of a hundred in the meeting hall normally used for the briefings. I had stated that I would hold as many meetings as necessary, until everyone had attended. Holding five meetings in three days on the same subject, with variously demanding audiences – the workforce proved more difficult than the managers with their questions – is especially testing. All the more so because those leaving were able to whisper to those entering those points that needed more explanation or replies that had not been satisfactory. Such an experience makes one aware of what I would call the physical side of communication. But there is no misunderstanding and the participants approve the 'performance' by paying incomparably closer attention than in any other situation. And ultimately everyone gains from it.

The large annual meeting of senior managers in the Agro sector was planned for mid October. You altered this meeting radically by inviting the participants to an actual reconfiguration of the company. How and why did this come about?

There were several reasons, but I no longer remember what order they came in.

At a methodological level I needed to bring people together to inform them about my project. In terms of the calendar, it was not easy to find a free period of time to do it. These dates were fixed; the temptation to use them was strong.

At the level of realism, it had to be admitted that to spend three days laying out the figures for 1994, plus 1995 and 1996 did not make much sense for a team whose initial target for the current year of FF1 bn of operational results had become FF700 m by mid May and down to FF500 m by mid September. We had lost our benchmarks and it was better to take note of it. On this score Tom Peters's caustic remarks were a great help.

Finally, in terms of communication, to announce that given the storm we found ourselves in, no-one, including ourselves, believed our figures any more, created an effect that gave credibility to the idea that I wanted to transmit of a 'culture shock'. Imagine the confusion of a financial controller who is told that there will be no budget and everyone in the company now only has one objective: to do better than last year – a concept of progress that remains essentially qualitative. In fact, no financial target was set for 1994, the only precise target being that for 1995: a FF500 m improvement in operational results compared with 1993. By breaking this taboo, I doubtless had the secret desire to get rid of the budget procedure for good. I did not succeed in this. While it has been simplified, it remains a Group exercise that appears to me to consume a disproportionate amount of time and energy compared with the presumed or real precision of the figures that emerge from it. Personally, I continue to prefer commitments to improvement based on growth targets defined by the accountable managers to the figures churned out by systems that render them anonymous and disconnected.

What makes you choose a process where you urge all the players to develop this reconfiguration of the company jointly?

It is first and foremost a profound conviction about the power of teamwork on the one hand, and about the ease of implementing shared decisions on the other. At the moment when I initiated SDM in September 1993, I had occasion to witness in another company a reorganization put together in a room by a group of seven persons: three consultants and four members of the executive board. One week before the public announcement of the project, the fifteen senior managers at level N–1 were given the 'privilege' of learning from the seven planners what the new organization was to be. It is scarcely worth mentioning that these managers spent the following months showing that the decisions that had been taken were not the right ones.

Quite frankly, I do not understand why one cannot choose the co-development route, once the directional line has been drawn. And to return briefly to the role of consultants, I do not understand in the case mentioned above how a reputable firm of consultants could back such an approach, even if the client requested it. In this case, the failure was such that the client was lost for a long time.

I would repeat that for me the question does not arise and co-development must be as broad as possible, if necessary including lower rank employees and staff from personnel.

Were the working groups a source of new ideas? How does the definitive project of April 1994 differ from that of October 1993?

So far as the broad principles were concerned, the project did not change fundamentally, but numerous improvements or additions were made. I have already talked about EVC which played an important role for SDM, Agro and the rest of the Group. In the area of organization, the working parties proposed and gained approval for the creation of 'internal enterprises' for the production of raw materials, operating with the same autonomy as the country units. This was something completely new which could only have been conceived by people on the ground.

The role of the head office had truly been restricted to the minimum, going beyond what I had imagined at the beginning of the process. It had become an obsession, witness this remark from Jean-René Fourtou whom I met by chance at a meeting in early 1994: 'Well, have you killed off the head office?'

The working groups set about the task and effectively reduced the head office to less than thirty people. The introduction of follow-up tools concerning the values and action principles is another achievement of the working parties. Finally, the 'social domain' group, as I have explained elsewhere, developed mutually accepted founding principles that today still govern employee and union relations in the company.

You turned the short term upside-down while sending out a mobilizing message on the long term and in particular on research. Can you say some more about how this key function was dealt with?

It was the 'Beaujolais group' that drew my attention to the fact that we had to make certain that the short-term approach took into account a long-term vision. It was not a neutral fact that middle management representatives requested this reinforcement of the message in the communication. This shows that on the ground people need vision. The official message about SDM was therefore strengthened to underline our will to be a leader in the profession: on the one hand by putting FF4 bn worth of new products on the market by the year 2000; on the other, by upgrading our research to adapt it to the needs of the market of 2010. This latter message was very reassuring for the 'social body'. It showed our will to be still there in 2010, which was what people wanted to hear in one way or another. In truth, I had not seen the impending arrival of the new technologies in all their fullness and the incorporation of this message in the SDM vision owes much to Philippe Desmarescaux who, as managing director and supervisor of the research group, was able to foresee the revolutions ahead through his contacts with the scientific world.

What I did was to seize upon this idea and put it up front in the internal communication, thus reassuring people, and to put all my weight behind its implementation in RP Agro. Thinking about the renewal of research was thus set in motion in parallel with the SDM project, without being an intrinsic part of it. It provided the researchers with a project too, and allowed them to question their approach to the development of key concepts for the future, such as high throughput screening and combinative chemistry. The fact that this process occurred in the same space-time as the implementation of SDM caused it to be assimilated into the SDM project. I allowed this amalgamation and no doubt even pressed for it to be perceived as such.

In all honesty, I would stress here that my personal involvement in the renewal of research was very different in nature from that in SDM. I was follower rather than promoter. Here again I took the opportunity offered to reinforce the message and the credibility of my own action.

This being the case, the scientific bonding achieved by the Rhône-Poulenc Agro research teams within two years was considerable, and research 'productivity', measured by the capacity for screening and the synthesis of new molecules, increased fifty times in two years, giving the prospect of identifying and developing the molecules that will be needed towards 2010, being used at the level of a few grammes per hectare and with total control over the environmental impact. This would undoubtedly be a chemical alternative to the biotechnological solutions that will be developed in parallel over the next decade and on which the agrochemical industry must position itself. But there we have another debate that may open a new page in the history of Rhône-Poulenc Agro.

During this construction phase, it seems to me that your role consists of ensuring the necessary protection of the process and being what I would call a resources provider.

It is true that while the working groups were busy, I lived through a kind of interlude, having little to do myself, in the *faber* sense of the term.

I was in close contact with the teams, encouraging, stimulating, clarifying when necessary. Quite often, people came to see me in order to understand better where I wanted to go and to be certain that they were working in the right direction. I also read many articles on management during this period because I needed to be reassured.

As I have explained elsewhere, the SDM approach was not unanimously seen to be good from the outside, and I had to defend it on several occasions. I did this more as a reinforcement for my colleagues than as an open offensive, except when I put my job on the line in order to be able to continue.

The energy that I had put into SDM was probably very perceptible to those around me, and I think that it naturally played the role of protection and reassurance that you mention.

The main resource that I represented for the team at Agro engaged in the action was probably more my conviction and my reassuring outward calmness than a methodological source, strictly speaking.

After the June 1994 conference, the new organization was put in place. What start-up problems did you encounter?

The start-up of the new organization took place without any particular problem, which does not mean that alterations were not needed here and there. For more than a year the cycle of thinking seminars on the topic 'enriching SDM' was in operation involving managers from around the globe twice in the year. The eighty of October 1993 had become one hundred and twenty through the addition of the heads of small subsidiaries, giving a group comprising more than 50 per cent non-French and twenty different nationalities.

The first part of the June 1994 conference had moreover got the participants to work on the subject. From their thoughts it emerged that priority should be given to 'across the board' communication and to the development of 'client actions' boosted by training. I had recruited a very young talented manager to present this last topic, with the assistance of specialized consultants.

Interesting ideas emerged, giving the head office the original role of promoting global politics that would nevertheless respect the autonomy of the decentralized units. Head office therefore implemented a subvention system (50 per cent of the contemplated budget) for the decentralized units to launch their 'client actions' (training, surveys, service quality assessment, and so on). The success of this approach was important and created a true movement of interest in the client, an interest measured by the social barometer in 1996.

One year and a half later, at the February 1996 international conference, I used a similar process to push the organization towards networking. From 1994 a system of global electronic communication (e-mail) had been introduced and the necessary investment obtained to ensure that units all around the world could communicate directly with one another, thus replacing the head office which had lost its role of central information distributor.

But I knew from my own numerous trips into the field that despite these tools, communication was bad when it came to certain topics that nevertheless needed to be shared. For example, comments made on our new insecticide Fipronil in Indonesia would have been very useful to our teams in Latin America. Travelling quite frequently from one continent to another within a single month, I saw that information did not circulate quickly enough, even though there was a demand for it on the ground. In February 1996, I decided to launch the idea of internal 'clubs', and to profit from the international conference to promote the concept of networking. My ideas came from what I had seen the previous year at the Davos symposium; I increased the number of tools for informal communication at the conference site and left sufficient time for contacts. Everyone was thus able to become aware of the importance of informal but fast communication on topics of common interest.

I then announced that every internal 'club' that was officially formed during the conference would receive an allocation of funds from head office for its implementation and the organization of the first meeting of its members. Thirteen clubs were formed in February 1996, opening the door to the start of a veritable 'across the board' networking that is so essential to a decentralized organization. Today there are 44 clubs and networks, involving more than 1700 persons which have added value to their tools with effective discussion forums that are widely used.

The seminars on 'how to enrich SDM' were also influential in the modification of some aspects of the initial SDM. For example, the management accounts section of the active principle units created some abnormal effects on the operation and decision-making of the managers. The remedy that was found facilitated the discovery of the right balance between the measurement of performance and the decision-making process. This was very important, because I consider that the functioning of the company is in fact a huge 'enterprise game'. One cannot play the 'game' well if a rule is inconsistent with the objective in view. Another decision that emerged from these thoughts was that of a return to an 'ethical and environmental' central function, which had been set aside in the drive for a head office that was as small as possible. Experience showed that the de-centralized units were not in a position to ensure this important function in a satisfactory manner, and when the players proposed that it should be reintegrated into head office, I accepted without hesitation.

But all this was merely fine-tuning in comparison with the organization that was advancing as planned and already showed its great efficiency and above all its 'joie de vivre'.

At these world conferences, how do you take into account the cultural differences in order to end up nevertheless with a common project?

The first thing to do is to be aware of these cultural differences and to be ever vigilant to the fact that some may have a completely different frame of reference. This is particularly true for Asians who must be shown special attention. We are more familiar with the faults and qualities of Anglo-Saxons, and Latin Americans do not have much difficulty in working with us.

The second thing is to ensure that the language is understood. At these meetings, English and French were the two official languages, with each person speaking his favourite tongue for immediate translation into the other one. Personal contact or small groups are also indispensable to ensure good understanding of the concepts and ideas.

The 'Orchids' programme, Agro's system of non-financial recognition, is a good example of the cross-cultural acceptance of a procedure that at the outset appears very American. Awards are generally made during international meetings and help to build a common team spirit.

One of the finest examples of intercultural communication that I have known occurred at the international conference of February 1996 at Aix-les-Bains. I had organized with Philippe Fournier, the young conductor of the Lyons Chamber Orchestra, an afternoon of musical recreation for the hundred and fifty participants. I had met Philippe Fournier some time previously and had been struck by his interest in music of course, but also by his interest in individuals and how they function as part of a team. He had developed some extraordinary exercises that allowed non-musicians to communicate thanks to the universal language of the body and music.

With the assistance of his musicians, he made everyone aware of the importance of listening and watching when communicating with others. It was a magical afternoon where everyone discovered the same mechanisms, irrespective of their cultural origins. Philippe Fournier has subsequently presented several seminars on this theme, with unfailing success. I would recommend the experience to those who like to link enjoyment and the discovery of differences with the pursuit of efficiency in a group.

More than four years afterwards, when you have ceased to be at the helm of Rhône-Poulenc Agro, what is your judgement on the evolution of your model?

Like any living thing, it adapts. Its foundations – the client, autonomy, EVC, pertinent cost, the importance of values – are still there, but as I had already begun to do, my successors must continue to add to it and make it evolve.

Some choices, such as the non-creation of a specific legal unit for distribution in France or the very dispersed location of buying in the organization, were the result of negotiations or hesitation where matters had to be settled quickly. The fact that these decisions were revised a few years later does not surprise me; quite the contrary. My message is to question and to adapt continually.

Another is the computer system for international logistics. When we decided on SDM, we were in the final stage of installation of an IT system designed for the centralized universe of 1991, the year in which a FF50m programme had been launched for it. This system was not on the main agenda in 1993–94; we simply made a few changes that were not the ideal solution, but everyone knew this.

A worldwide system, suitable for a decentralized organization and designed with the strong involvement of all units and clients, is currently in the course of development. This is an undeniable advance that will nevertheless noticeably affect certain processes.

I have discussed the subject of the evolution of organizations at length with Claude Michaud, director of CEDEP, who leads research with Jean-Claude Thoenig on management models. He defines two, which he calls 'income creator' and 'income exploiter'. Having closely studied the SDM operation on the basis of numerous interviews between 1994 and 1998, he defined it very clearly as an 'income creation', that is, the construction of a substantial asset that puts its stamp on the company and which should be exploited at length.

In a sense, my successors – the management team at Agro has been substantially altered in recent years – have as their mission to 'exploit' this income, that is literally to make the business profitable, without forgetting that their mission is also to improve constantly and be ready one day to invent something else to enable the business to follow its path. For this is how companies advance, evolving periodically and by stages, with each new project taking over the baton from the preceding ones, sometimes to build something very different, but which would not have existed in this form without the previous creators.

As Saint-Exupéry said in words that I remember well, having been given them as an essay topic at my *baccalauréat*: 'To be a man is to be responsible. It is to be aware, as you place your stone, that you have made your contribution to building the world ...' I find that these words apply perfectly to business and to the roles of those who engage in it; they make one feel both proud and modest, two qualities that are essential for long-term success.

2 Stakes and Convictions

In 1993, we saw the different parameters that brought about an internal crisis for you. What options did you have?

First there are the so-called external solutions, making alliances or agreements with third parties. At the time the world agrochemical industry had been going through a decade of consolidation. This movement has moreover continued since and has not stopped with the new challenge posed by the plant biotechnologies.

In 1993, there were several options of external alliances for Rhône-Poulenc Agro, either global or partial, which would have had a positive impact in improving the results through the classic effects of synergy.

I had the merger/agreement models for our most interesting competitors updated. But a time of crisis is not the best moment to bring off a successful merger. Such procedures require time to mature and their prime objective must be strategic reinforcement in the long term rather than the solution of a climatic economic crisis. These files would probably have been reopened if no internal solution had been found, which was fortunately not the case.

The internal solutions were of two types. The traditional solutions were to reduce operating costs by huge restructuring, perhaps together with the recombining of portfolios eliminating the less profitable products. They have proved effective in numerous situations, especially as first line solutions. They are in fact subject to the law of diminishing profits that makes them lose their return if they are used repeatedly. People greatly underestimate the 'joule effect' generated in such cases on the technical and psychological levers which these methods warrant. Nevertheless, the remarks from the executive board had directed me towards this route of reducing turnover and fixed costs.

The solutions described as 'coming out through the top' are aimed at creating value from a reaction and mobilization of the human resources of the company. Such solutions are more risky, and any failure is more easily attributable, and therefore punishable. This is perhaps why they occur less frequently than the others do.

One is strategic and defensive; the other dynamic and offensive. The Maginot line against the Arcole bridge.

For myself, I did not believe in the first category anymore in the context of Rhône-Poulenc Agro, and the 'other thing' that I sought led me inevitably to 'coming out through the top'. That is, finding the right ingredients for the solution to take account of the economic aspects that remain inescapable, but trying to base them on the foundations and the human potential of the company.

What forms the basis of your convictions?

Thinking about these with hindsight, I believe that at heart I have always preferred human beings to systems. The unique model, and the certainty it brings with it that it is 'the' best option, makes me uncomfortable and I have difficulty in going along with it.

It is the first time in my career that I have had the opportunity to escape it by developing my own idea and my own solution. I am first of all driven by a feeling of rebellion. The remainder – the book by Tom Peters, my contact with Jean-René Fourtou and the 'Beaujolais group' – only strengthened my first conviction that was above all personal.

How did your internal environment at Rhône-Poulenc receive this approach?

At the beginning, I was prudent in the way I presented it, insisting on a reduction of staff at head office, without revealing that it did not necessarily imply in my mind a global reduction in staff. In fact, a number of transfers from head office to the decentralized units or to service units will limit the number of lost jobs. But it seemed preferable to me to retain the ambiguity. So much so that a few months later, when I was announcing a reduction of thirty-nine jobs at the meeting to close the project, some people, remembering from my initial presentation that it was an operation to reduce fixed costs (head office was going from five hundred staff to less than thirty), showed clearly that the mountain was labouring to bring forth a mouse.

There were no problems with the qualitative aspects of the project – decentralization, autonomy, subsidiarity, values – given that they were supported by Jean-René Fourtou. As for the remainder, my own firm commitment to double the results within two years was sufficient to reassure everyone. But it took a year, as success dawned, for the last sceptics to decide to fly to the aid of victory.

I note that the recurrent connection that you make between the social and the economic is central for you in the success of SDM and, in more general way, in your management style.

I discovered the importance of social dialogue in Portugal, in 1975, in the middle of the 'carnation' revolution. I was then managing director of Agrop, the Portuguese subsidiary of Rhône-Poulenc Agro. Events were dragging the country into a largely uncontrollable situation: labour demands, strikes, questioning of country leaders, expulsion of landowners, collapse of the currency, import restrictions, and so on.

While factories were closing one after the other, Agrop was one of the rare companies in its industrial area to avoid a strike, thanks to a negotiation session with the totally new 'workers commission'. On that day, I became aware that the social could not be separated from the economic and that the one nurtured the other. Through its workers commission, the workforce claimed an immediate 50 per cent salary increase for everyone. Armed with diagrams, I spent a large part of the day explaining to my claimants that these salary demands were putting the survival of the company at stake. All the more so because the company, given its seasonal activity, would not be able to withstand a strike during a key production period.

I explained the probable scenario to them. I would return to a comfortable job in France and the operations in Portugal would be closed down. This eventuality was all the more credible because the head office had just withdrawn its bank surety and required payments to be made by irrevocable and confirmed letters of credit, which obliged me to embark on a new set of gymnastics with the local banks.

By the middle of the afternoon, the members of the commission were convinced to accept my proposition. This was simple: if we were to avoid a strike, we should have to sell more, since the majority of our competitors had ceased operations. We might then not only attain our targets, but exceed them. A quick calculation of the positive impact of such a situation allowed me to offer a 10 per cent salary increase and a bonus of one month's salary if a new growth target was achieved.

At the time there was little interest from workers in a company's financial results and even less in Portugal than elsewhere. The four members of the commission nonetheless agreed to present my proposition for the workers to vote on. At around 8.00 pm, after three hours of discussions which I later learnt were stormy, they came to inform me that the proposition was accepted, on one condition which I did not think it useful to discuss further. This condition was that it should be up to the commission to decide how the 10 per cent for the workforce was to be distributed; this turned out to be a uniform salary for all employees, except that the men were to receive 8000 escudos, while the women received 7000. The revolution still had some way to go!

Subsequently, between 1987 and 1995, I had to conduct numerous negotiations on restructuring, merging networks, factory closures and of course social plans. In these discussions, the trade unions were always provided with the maximum information, often strategic, in order to understand and analyse the data of the problem in question.

Respect for people at whatever level, transparency, conviction and straight talking have always been the permanent ingredients of these negotiations and social dialogue. The advantages of such an approach for everyone are clear. As the CFDT union representative of Rhône-Poulenc Agro said concerning SDM in an interview with the newspaper *Le Monde*[1]: 'We were integrated into the process upstream, which explains why today, we have acquired a negotiation culture that did not exist in the rest of the Group.' For me, social dialogue is indeed an element of value creation for the company, to which modern managers should give all their attention. It is nevertheless a fragile element that takes a long time to build and can deteriorate in a very short time.

The 'social barometer' allows you, among other things, to identify and promote a certain number of values. Do I understand correctly that you were constantly concerned to translate these values into management principles and action?

Holding values (and not just any values) seems to me to be indispensable, in life and in a business. In a business, affirming values with a precise commitment lets everyone know where they stand. It is a first step.

But putting them into practice is another story. In a group of people, some will believe strongly in one value and not especially in another. Their behaviour will show the effects of it and, at the end of the line, the basic level employees will be inclined to think that this stuff about company values has little to do with them. Furthermore, one must recognize that directors of companies are sometimes faced with situations similar to what one might call 'company reasons' by analogy with 'reasons of state'. These situations require flexible attitude with regard to certain affirmed values. Those who wish to carry this concept of company values deeply into their organization must first find the modesty to recognize that these values are not applied 100 per cent, and they probably never will be. What is at stake is to encourage those behaviours that contribute to reducing the gap between what is affirmed on the one hand and practiced on the other. My own experience suggests that people prefer to detect this mixture of weakness and goodwill in their superiors, rather than the somewhat arrogant certainty that they encounter most often on this type of subject. In this sense, the social barometer or the management questionnaire, because they sometimes provide disturbing responses, are interesting tools for managers who believe in them. Their regular and virtually obligatory use in a modern management organization signifies above all that there is a will at executive level to be questioned and to advance. So far as values are concerned, this is often the main one.

You have paid special attention to relations with the unions and with employee representatives.

Yes, because once again I have a conviction forged by experience in this field. For me economic efficiency in the long term requires high quality social dialogue; that is, each party must respect the other.

As it is still too rarely the case on all sides, too few young people dare to become involved in trades unions, whereas companies clearly need them in order to manage change. Some unions have begun their renewal process and are becoming demanding but responsible negotiators that are appreciated by the employers. The remainder should be helped to progress rather than be rejected and marginalized. The men and women who form their membership are generally of high quality and ready to call into question those institutions that have come from a period that they privately recognize as outmoded.

I am of those who believe that the unions should be stronger and more representative than they are today. My strategy of involving them positively in the thinking on SDM is rooted in this conviction, and follows from numerous similar situations where, in one form or another, they played the role of constructive partners. This does not exclude firmness when necessary, as was the case when I refused to allow them to participate in the October 1993 seminar, despite a request supported by a petition signed by more than two hundred.

If dignity and respect are perceived on both sides, it is much easier to accept the reasons for a refusal and calmly continue negotiation. Of course, one must not be naïve and understand that there is a union game to be played out; so room must be left for its view to be expressed when it must be done, without there necessarily being an outcome.

I consider that French management trainee culture does not prepare managers well for modern trade union relations. However, a personal anecdote makes me believe that it would not take much to change things.

In 1992, elections of employee representatives were due to take place. The usual level of participation for the management constituency was of the order of 20 per cent, as in most companies incidentally. At the briefing that took place before the elections, I gave out a message on the necessity in these difficult times to have strong union partners and reminded the managers of their responsibility: 'Voting for the elections to the CCE (Central Committee of the company, where unions are represented) is part of your mission, as is persuading your teams to go and vote. It is a question of ability to push things forward in the company.' The result of this short but forceful campaign of awareness was that the participation level rose to more than 50 per cent, allowing the management constituency to be elected on the first round, which had never happened before.

In your profession, cohabitation of the short term with the long term is essential. What were your concerns with regard to research during this period?

In businesses where innovation is a key success factor, when a crisis is encountered there is serious anxiety among the researchers because they are always fearful that their budgets will be the first to be cut. Any alteration, even minor, is thus perceived as a desire on the part of management to cut down on research, therefore to favour the short term compared with the long term.

It was a major danger in the SDM process, which called for a rapid improvement in the financial results. All the more because the French researchers, who were demotivated, were strongly criticized by their commercial colleagues, who for no reason saw them as responsible for their difficulties. The 'Beaujolais group' was the first to draw my attention to this danger, and they insisted on our long-term vision in the report. When a little later, under the aegis of Philippe Desmarescaux, it appeared that new technologies – combinative chemistry, miniaturization of screening tests, robotization, and so on – might revolutionize the work of researchers, I called upon them to invest in this project and to reconstruct their approach themselves. This was a process very similar to that of SDM, which incidentally became completely assimilated into people's spirit, but which developed in parallel. My merit lay in taking advantage of this opportunity that came from outside in order to offer the researchers the direction that they needed to conduct their mission and which they could not find sufficiently clearly in the general SDM project. From that moment, I engaged broadly with them in their thinking, never overlooking any occasion to recognize publicly their efforts and worth.

This 'protection' of the researchers was essential to restore in them the necessary confidence for their difficult mission. And it should be recognized that today, the work of questioning and renewal that the researchers gave themselves up to have placed Rhône-Poulenc Agro at the forefront of advanced technological research into new molecules.

3 Personal Motives

At the age of forty-seven, when you began this adventure, I imagine you felt ready to tackle it. What prepared you for it?

At that time I already had more than twenty-five years of professional experience, including some very impressive times which moulded and hardened me. I am in the habit of saying that I passed through four schools in my professional life before SDM.

The first is my course in agronomics at the Toulouse National Agronomics College. Strictly speaking, this is not a '*grande école*' (in the special sense understood by the French establishment), but a school of engineers which quickly opened the gates to my professional life. I had chosen it basically in order to save time, since its competitive entry required just one year of preparation after the *baccalauréat* in science which I had also chosen as an easier option, being a little weak in mathematics. Knowing and recognizing one's weaknesses is a strength in building one's career. I learnt a little about a lot, but it gave me a general scientific knowledge of life sciences which has effectively helped me throughout my career.

My second school is Africa. After being taken on at the end of my studies by IRHO (Institute of Research into Oils and Oilseeds) as a researcher, I was given the additional task of being responsible for the administration of the Pobé station (Bénin) to which I had been posted in 1967. There I learnt about budgets, administrative procedures and managing people. The station comprised three hundred hectares of palm oil plantation, a factory, research laboratories for variety selection and employed several hundred people including six expatriates. Thanks to my recently gained knowledge of administrative matters I had the good fortune to be appointed acting managing director of this organization for two months. At the age of twenty-two, I learnt the basics and practice of management and leadership at a level that would have taken me years to achieve elsewhere. I returned to France in 1969 where I joined the American company Rohm and Haas which taught me soil agriculture, sales and marketing.

Expatriated in 1972 to Portugal, I found my third school in 1975 when I joined the Rhône-Poulenc Group. As managing director of a subsidiary cut off from head office in the middle of the 'carnation revolution', I had in fact to manage a truly autonomous small business in a very unstable environment and to find solutions at all levels: financial, social, technical, commercial, and so on. I was under thirty and this was the toughest of my schools.

My fourth school was the acquisition of Union Carbide by Rhône-Poulenc Agro in 1986–87. This was not an easy file, but Philippe Desmarescaux felt from the start that it was the opportunity that he had been seeking for some years. He was able to convince Jean-René Fourtou who had just become chairman of the Group and who plunged us into the adventure.

I can remember the meeting he called on the day before the signature: 'We are committing our future, double or quits. I need you behind me for we shall be embarking on a period of effort and commitment that transcends anything we have known up to now.' We were behind him in his bid to succeed in this gamble and I learnt much about people in the light of the role of committed and demanding captain that Philippe Desmarescaux played in order to make us give of our best.

Apart from the lesson in management and the strategic approach, I also learnt a great deal about methodology and I discovered the Americans. They brought rigour, the importance of the concept of contractual commitment, and they made us improve the quality of our briefs. The merging process itself constituted top class training, of the type to build for the future. If I also add to these four significant periods of my professional life the flying hours of these twenty-six years, which enabled me to discover more than fifty countries with their different cultures, to experience the complexities of agricultural development and finance, of setting up subsidiaries, of negotiating at all levels, I would consider myself prepared to face the crisis before me.

An important factor for success in SDM is unquestionably your capacity to speak in public. Where does this talent come from?

Like most people, I get stage fright before every public appearance. But I enjoy fighting it and overcoming it. For this reason, apart from internal communication, which is relatively easy when you know whom you are talking to, I have always responded to the most hazardous invitations, such as live television debates or public staged events. Where does this ability come from, talent being probably too strong a word, because I always do my personal preparation? I think a psychologist would give a better answer. Like many people, I was very timid as a child, but I had the luck to see very quickly the power of humour and spectacle to counterbalance this excessive sensitivity. Having an audience permits one to 'exist'. Stories and songs learnt by heart, then later the gift of mimicry, songwriting and singing allowed me more than anything to open up and round off my personality.

One has to look at these precocious experiments of my adolescence, that later gave way to an ability to organize fêtes and events, in order to discover my liking, then as now, for communicating, especially through public speaking.

Did you seriously contemplate the possibility of failure in this adventure?

For a long time – and this has certainly played a role in my career – I have believed in my lucky star, and I belong to that group of people to whom others have the tendency to entrust difficult tasks, simply because 'he has luck on his side'. This did not prevent me, well before 1993, from preparing myself intellectually to face up to a career accident and steeling myself in order to live through it undamaged if it did arise. I have often seen 'high flyers' turn into losers simply as a consequence of being close to a business or organization in a bad state of health, as a result of decisions taken by others.

One needs to get one's head well above this type of situation and this can be prepared for by thinking about oneself and about others on the one hand, and by life and commitment outside the company on the other. Too many managers live only through their companies and, as Olivier Lecerf[2] reminds us, do not make a distinction between what is important (the business) and what is essential (life). Such people do not survive well through a professional crisis – even retirement, and are not more effective.

During the implementation of SDM, I was well aware that I was gambling my career. Everyone, above and below me, also knew it. I was also convinced that I was engaging in a fine and fair cause that I had chosen myself. At the professional level, if I did not see the struggle through to the end I would 'fall' with the satisfaction of having done my duty, and I would not have suffered at the personal level.

I was aware of my abilities and I was not worried about having to start up again if that had been necessary. All the more so since at my level of responsibility, one has a useful financial cushion to permit one to reorganize the future if need be. When in March 1994 I put my mission into play, I knew what I was doing. It was a decision that had been thought through, assumed as a responsibility and discussed in advance with my wife. I was calm and ready for anything – but I would have preferred not to have had to live through this situation at all.

You indicate that in the framework of the new decentralized organization you have established positive and negative sanctions that are stronger than previously.

Empowerment does in fact lead to a more assertive system of sanctions than in a centralized organization where the rule is to open an umbrella as protection against any problem. People who found themselves pushed into key positions in the new set-up are the most exposed: if they do not deliver the spreading of EVC, which is the rule of the game, they find themselves in a weakened position which may lead to their removal (this has happened).

This type of decision is difficult to take. Apart from the figures, one must take account of the abilities and the environment, and that remains very subjective. The few examples that have affected Rhône-Poulenc Agro were not accepted unanimously, but they sent a strong message as to the riskiness of certain jobs that hitherto were regarded as protected. On the other hand, variable remuneration packages that are extremely attractive have been developed for these posts. Taking together in general the annual performance and a measure of the cumulative improvement over three years, this means that some managers can achieve an additional variable remuneration of 50 per cent of their basic salary.

Having put these managers in place, I had to defend them before the Group head of Human Resources who considered these sums of money to be too high for the level of position. But for me these entrepreneurial posts were the key to the system and I was able to convince my colleagues of this.

That said, recognition is not only measured by money. One of the great successes of Rhône-Poulenc Agro is the 'Orchids' scheme organized every two years to honour the most worthy teams and individuals. Launched in 1990 at the suggestion of the Anglo-Saxons who are great enthusiasts of these awards, the scheme was rejuvenated with the implementation of SDM which decentralized the selection process and created awards linked to objectives in tune with the principles of action, always with the aim of focusing everyone's attention on values.

Silver orchids and gold orchids became a component of the life of Rhône-Poulenc Agro, appealing world-wide to all players in the company – managers, office staff, workers – including the French, who were wary of this 'gimmick' at the beginning. In 1998, 797 people, representing 92 teams, entered as candidates. Forty-five silver orchids and seven gold orchids were awarded, the latter being presented formally at the international conference. The pride and pleasure of the winners are a gift for them, but also for the whole company.

You give priority to the process of implementation in the real world by seeking above all coherence between speech and practice and by encouraging the model role for managers.

It must be admitted that it is not natural to talk about values in a company, especially at the beginning. However, it is fundamental, as J.C. Collins and J.I. Porras remind us in their excellent book *Built to Last*.[3] Here they characterize visionary enterprises as those that have known how to develop this essential coherence between speech and action. The commitment of the top executive is the first step in the process, transmitted onwards by those close to him who must feel that they are participating completely in order for 'something to happen'. Tools come next, as an element of communication and dissemination, influencing individual and collective behaviour. The management questionnaire played this role in SDM and remains a tool still in active use and even expected by the teams. What had been interesting in the procedure that I had conducted, was that it was adopted as a whole by the Group, largely due to the influence of Jean-René Fourtou who was waiting for an opportunity to push this concept. Today, future managers are evaluated with the help of two main criteria: their ability to deliver the expected results on the one hand, and their way of promoting the values and principles for action on the other. For me, this generalization of the principle of the balance between the economic and the human is a great victory that has recently become institutionalized at Group level in a document destined to all managers (Figure 2.1).

What is important in a matter such as this, is the effect that it has on people's

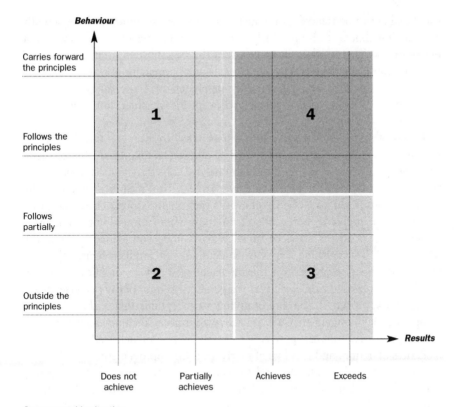

Figure 2.1 *Assessment grid for managers in the Rhône-Poulenc Group*

behaviour, for it is this that causes things to change. It is a sign of considerable progress to be able to talk with future managers of the Group and to tell them that apart from being effective players at the economic level, they need to invest as much energy in those who will achieve tomorrow's successes, namely people.

How would you summarize the key points of your reference framework for the organization?

Two key concepts seem to me to require taking into account increasingly by modern organizations: the management of uncertainties and that of contradictions. Now, our educational and training systems, especially the French systems that place strong emphasis on the training of engineers and on the certainties and rigidities that follow from it, do not prepare people very well for this new complexity. Too many managers and people in charge have the tendency to lay down the law without hesitation in the name of the truth that seems quite obvious to them. From the moment I accept that the economic and the social are to be treated with equal worth in the organization, I am actually announcing that a decision which is obvious from one point of view is not necessarily so from another viewpoint, that the two shutters are interactive and that the solution to implement is the result of a permanent unstable balancing act. When I preach the participative approach and the autonomy in an organization, I am aware that such concepts have their limits in certain situations.

I must be in a position to explain it and to say to everyone that I, too, live with my own contradictions and I must be allowed to take ownership of them. This candid attitude is essential to maintain the consistency of a company, and therefore to allow everyone to carry with them the 'meaning' given to the business, even in the face of one-off events that might contradict it. Accepting uncertainty is probably more difficult for those who surround entrepreneurs – senior managers, shareholders, financial analysts, and so on – since the IT world, which controls everything, urges us increasingly to produce figures that are presumed correct simply because they have emerged from a complicated system.

The example of setting objectives is a good illustration of the perverse effects of such an approach. To be sure of giving an acceptable figure, that is, in the company's view a figure that will be achieved, seasoned commercial managers set low objectives that are quite easy to reach. This approach leads to a certain facileness of action, and to a loss of motivation for improvement.

To overcome this difficulty and to manage objectives in a motivating way while acknowledging uncertainty, I have developed a system based on three levels:

- *Commitment*, corresponding to what is reasonably achievable;
- *Hope*, which takes into account favourable factors linked to external events;
- *Dream*, adding to hopes what might be developed on parts identified but not yet worked on, if everything goes as well as it could.

This approach, which is incorporated in the book's title, when used to manage the growth of new products has proved extremely effective and motivating, allowing this problem to be tackled in an entertaining rather than a stressful way.

With four years of hindsight, I can confirm that the sales achieved for a product like Fipronil are today closer to the 'dreams' than the 'commitments' set at the time (see Figure 3.8b on p. 81).

Notes

1. 'Rhône-Poulenc Agrochimie reaps the rewards of its decentralization', *Le Monde*, 26 March 1998.
2. Oliver Lecerf, Philippe de Woot and Jacques Barraux, *Au Risque de Gagner*, Paris: Éditions de Fallois, 1991.
3. James C. Collins and Jerry I. Porras, *Bâties pour Durer: les Enterprises Visionnaires ont-elles un Secret?* (*Built to Last – The Secret of Visionary Enterprises*), Paris: First, 1996.

PART 3

The Present and the Future

Vincent Lenhardt with comments from Alain Godard

Visual Synthesis of Part 3: Handling the Cursor

This table shows a visual synthesis of Part 3. Taking as starting point a macroeconomic and global perception of the two worlds (industrial and post-industrial), it sketches the logical basis that underpins them and the organizations that represent them.

Then follow the development stages of the teams and the individual managerial identities that flow from them.

Finally, it is not simply a question of moving from one world to another, but of managing permanently the coexistence of these two worlds, with the contradictions arising from ambiguity and the paradoxes that result from these. The difficulty in moving the cursor represents the price to be paid by managers in passing through the complexity.

| **Macroeconomic level** |
| Approach |
| Logic |
| Organization |

| **Stages of team development** |

| **Managerial personality** |

| **Stages of growth** |

| **The cursor** |

World of industrial era	World of postmodern era
• Planning • Target	• Constructivism • Emergence
Order and obedience	Co-responsibility
Taylorian and mechnical	Systematic and complex

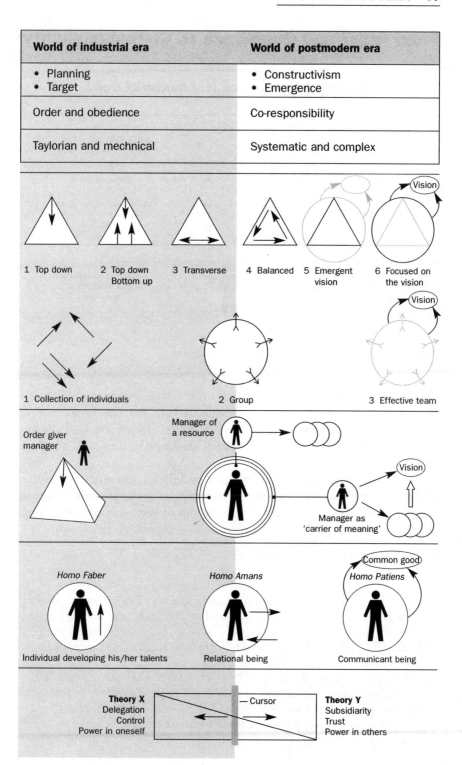

1 Top down   2 Top down Bottom up   3 Transverse   4 Balanced   5 Emergent vision   6 Focused on the vision

1 Collection of individuals   2 Group   3 Effective team

Order giver manager   Manager of a resource   Manager as 'carrier of meaning'   Vision

Homo Faber   *Homo Amans*   *Homo Patiens*   Common good

Individual developing his/her talents   Relational being   Communicant being

Theory X
Delegation
Control
Power in oneself

— Cursor

Theory Y
Subsidiarity
Trust
Power in others

From Order and Obedience to Co-responsibility

1 The shock of the industrial and post-industrial world

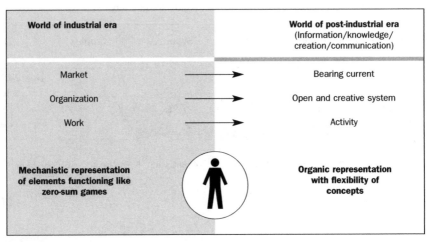

Figure 3.1 *Players destabilized between two worlds*

From now on every business is involved on one level in two worlds: that of the industrial era and that of the post-industrial era. Markets, organizations, the workplace and consequently the identities of the players (individuals, teams, institutions) are conditioned by parameters from these two worlds at one and the same time.

Forces and laws ruling these two worlds and their coexistence are sources of what is called the universe of complexity (not anymore that of complication). They threaten to surround the players with contradictions, double constraints, paradoxes and permanent and unyielding ambiguities.

The following boxed comments in this section are from Alain Godard.

> I believe that the majority of managers have understood that we are entering a new world that you describe as post-industrial, and admit that this world is indeed filled with uncertainty. The ambiguity stems from the fact that they want to tackle this world with the tools from the industrial world, because these are tools that they know and are happy with.
>
> Now, when I consider a new technology such as the plant biotechnologies, I can confirm that they will play a major role in the agriculture of tomorrow and change our profession, but I am unable to establish the sacrosanct business plan which, according to our systems, will trigger the allocation of resources to invest in them and prepare our future.

We can feel that this new world obliges us to take a chance based rather on convictions arising from scientific facts and an analysis of society's evolution than from a traditional payback calculation.

Nevertheless, in this new profession, full of unknowns and uncertainties, financial analysts continue to make use of financial ratios produced from figures calculated to two or three decimal places. That illustrates how difficult the transitions are.

2 Management in chaos and complexity

The managerial situation must from now on conform to external reality where uncertainty appears most immediately evident. From this it follows that the managers' functioning is conditioned by how they manage their relationship with perfection, both their own and that of others.

Fear and guilt are the feelings that are bound to be found in the management of chaos because nothing turns out as expected. There are then two possible attitudes:

- Either one adopts a defensive approach, spending one's time opening the umbrella, justifying to oneself and avoiding anything risky because one cannot allow oneself to make a mistake; or
- One gives oneself the right to make a mistake and emerges from the dichotomy of failure–success into the coupling of 'attempt and adjust'. Our position is to invite all managers to consider in their values that they must, without trying to make mistakes, take at least 20 per cent of calculated risks. Otherwise, they would only be doing the things that they know perfectly and which are in fact quite likely to lock them into a routine. It would not be long before they became condemned dinosaurs in a constantly changing world. Acceptance of uncertainty and of a certain amount of imperfection is one of the gateways to the management of chaos. The manager must learn to be comfortable with ambiguity, ambivalence, paradox, frustration and capacity for change, which are the inescapable constituent elements for the management of chaos.

By *ambiguity* we mean the continual presence of different levels of reality and meaning that we have mentioned earlier. For example, if the manager has to conduct a meeting, it is perhaps more important for the meeting to be longer than planned and not terminate with an operational decision, if the outcome is to unblock a psychological conflict between two persons who were holding up the team's work; or if this meeting allows a power struggle to be resolved, or a team member on the sidelines to be reintegrated.

As we shall see later in greater detail, the manager is destined to manage continually the ambiguity between the content and the process. It is not a

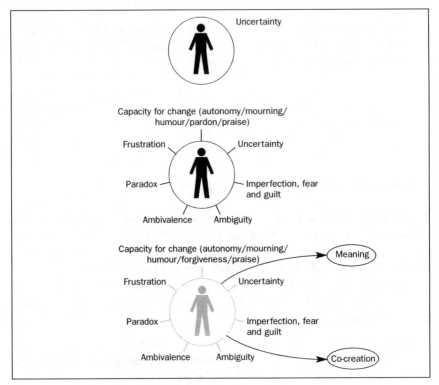

Figure 3.2 *The management of chaos*

question of two contradictory realities but of two polarities between which managerial reality is constantly located.

By *ambivalence* we mean the fundamental contradiction that every manager must resolve, namely to want something and its opposite. He wants to be seen as the boss and at the same time he wants his subordinates to function when he is not there. He wants his team to have ideas without him and at the same time he is unhappy that his ideas are not accepted without question. He wants his colleagues to take initiatives with his internal and external clients, but he does not like his clients to deal with anyone but him.

By *paradox* we are thinking of the role of the manager who, the more he wants to go in one direction, the more important it is for him to be tactful in saying what he wants in order to avoid any rejection or blocking on the part of his colleagues.

Tom Peters, in his book on the management of chaos,[1] points to a set of eighteen paradoxes that need to be mastered in the area of change. We shall quote three:

- The more importance one attaches to the quality of a product, the more one needs to detach oneself from the product itself in order to face up to the necessary technological change.

- The more intense the change imposed by the exercise of one's profession, the more necessary it is to find strong stable areas, such as for example confidence in the team that one belongs to and security of employment.
- Finally, the paradox that seems to us to be the most important one to be managed is as follows: if I want to keep some control of the situation, I must basically give up any idea of too constraining a control.

By *frustration* we mean that the manager shows his real ability to manage chaos. Is he capable of surviving the inevitable frustrations generated by the constant gaps between real situations and wished-for situations?

By *capacity for change* we are referring to a number of qualities that the manager must possess, such as for example autonomy which we have already discussed, his ability to abandon lost causes, a certain humour which allows him to defuse situations and which testifies to a position of meta-communication, together with a forgiving attitude as much towards others as towards himself.

All of these elements are aspects of the chaos in which the manager mainly evolves. He can only take charge of this chaos by endowing it with a 'meaning', of which he is the bearer through his 'vision'. This organizational and individual meaning is made up of values and objectives which inspire him, from a profoundly existential and spiritual viewpoint that is ever present, even if it is repressed or not yet recognized.

The manager who is now bearer of the meaning, both for himself and for those for whom he is responsible, can now feel at one with himself and see his actions move from the absurdity of chaos to a perspective of creation, or rather co-creation, with others and with what lies at the heart of his spirituality or his beliefs.

Management in a world full of certainty was ultimately easy. The signposts supported by figures that could be relied upon showed the way reassuringly. What I often notice in my company is the difficulty in replacing this reassuring sign-posting with the concept of 'meaning', an indicator that is naturally much more qualitative.

As for myself, before launching SDM, I did not talk sufficiently about meaning and I insist on this signpost of two years, plus FF500 bn operational results. It is the 'Beaujolais group' consisting of middle management that insists on the fact that my approach should be refocused on the long-term perspective, by defining objectives in the field of research, for example. This shows that these operational managers are not taken in, are aware of the complexity in which we find ourselves and are ready to follow me if this vision is made to take in the long-term view; this becomes for them the reassuring element that prompts them to lend their support.

3 Passage from one logic to another

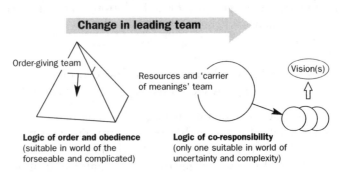

Figure 3.3 *Need to move from one logic to another*

There is the need to move from the Taylorian logic where a few can think (senior executives and experts) and others practise obediently, to the logic that everyone thinks and practises: the logic of co-responsibility. This requires fundamental change in the structures, systems, visions, identities and roles of the senior executives. They have to move from the role of order giver (OG), controller and decider, to a role that is both resource manager (RM) and carrier of meaning (CM), that is, 'giver', 'listener' and 'shower' of the meaning.

> When at the beginning I explained what I wanted to do with SDM, I used the metaphor of the umbrella and the flag. 'Let's leave the umbrellas in the lobby, and take hold of the flags...' This indicated clearly in my mind that the centralized system, which largely stands for a logical order, did not allow autonomy and responsibility to emerge.
>
> With hindsight, I have been surprised at the facility with which the majority of the players have found their place in the new decentralized organization and have assumed their new managerial responsibility.
>
> This would suggest that this evolution corresponds to a true expectation of the players, and that the process can develop further in the business.

4 Passage from the 'pill' vision to the 'jointly developed' vision

Moving from one logic to another presupposes another way of perceiving the vision(s) and for the managers a fundamental and lasting questioning of their systems of representation and of their processes for developing visions. They will also need to invest considerably in communication, listening and support for everyone to have his or her say.

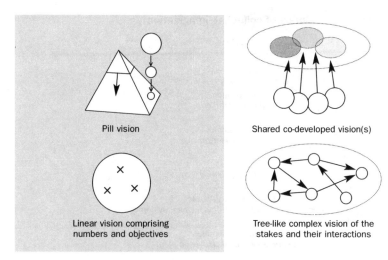

Figure 3.4 *Two types of vision*

As an analogy, let us take the steering of a liner or a large warship where the commander may take the helm. When it is a question of a flotilla of ships of different sizes, this same commander can no longer take the helm of each of these ships. He has to define the global headland and ensure that each person in charge of a ship is able to sail on while maintaining convoy position. We should remember the important rule of complex systems: management of a complex system can only be conducted with the agreement of the parties to its ends (this is what is meant by 'management by meaning').

I remember the first exercise in which Rhône-Poulenc Agro tried to establish its vision for the future. All the managers were summoned to air their thoughts about this as a participative process. There was a long debate to establish whether we saw ourselves as *the* leader in the profession – a view held by a minority – or *one* of the leaders – the view held by the vast majority of the players.

Philippe Desmarescaux, then managing director and more in favour of the first view of the company, nevertheless came down in favour of the second, because he was aware that in order to be accepted and experienced as a reality, the largest number of people must share the vision. There was even more reason for him to do it in order to mobilize the teams, even though he personally thought otherwise.

5 Logical levels of the vision (space and time)

One can only speak of shared vision(s) if each player can see the 'stone in the cathedral wall'. The diagram in Figure 3.5 shows how the same problem must be handled differently (for example, resource allocation or client

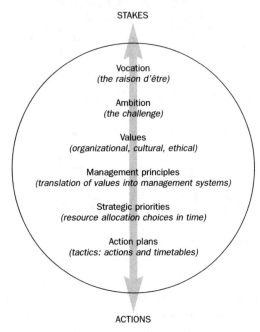

Space of collective imagination

STAKES

Vocation
(the raison d'être)

Ambition
(the challenge)

Values
(organizational, cultural, ethical)

Management principles
(translation of values into management systems)

Strategic priorities
(resource allocation choices in time)

Action plans
(tactics: actions and timetables)

ACTIONS

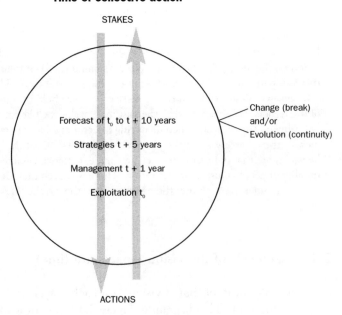

Time of collective action

STAKES

Forecast of t_0 to $t + 10$ years

Strategies $t + 5$ years

Management $t + 1$ year

Exploitation t_0

Change (break)
and/or
Evolution (continuity)

ACTIONS

Figure 3.5 *Logical levels of the vision*

relations) depending on whether the player is acting in the very short term (for example, economic cuts, responding to a client) or in the long term (investing or preparing business plans, training, travelling). The director must keep a kind of 'managerial yoyo' permanently in play, between these different logical levels that operate in apparent contradiction or what we may call 'dialogues' (that is, logics of different ranks that nonetheless coexist). The ambiguity and paradox of these contradictions has to be managed continuously and it is necessary to move from 'or' to 'and'. Some examples are: integrating the short and long terms, action and reflection, the individual and the business, speaking and listening, work on the ground and the objectivity benefits of training, and so on.

The role of the meaning-bearing managers is to incline permanently towards building a coherence for themselves and for others that is at one and the same time personal, organizational and company-wide. The creation of values presupposes that everyone, so far as possible, is a winner: shareholders, workers, managers, clients, suppliers and those in the surrounding environment.

I had much difficulty in getting our American teams to accept this double constraint of the short term and the long term at the beginning of the 1990s. Their more structured and contractual approach brought forth more clear-cut responses than ours, because they are less able to live in an ambiguous world than us Latins.

The time it took us to organize and bring our American team into line bears witness to this difficulty that Americans have in accepting contradictory objectives.

6 The Minimal Shared Cultural Envelope (MSCE)

The creation of shared visions goes far beyond the simple sharing of figures, ratios or operational objectives. It presupposes a mutual exchange and a common approach that ensures agreement on the six parameters of Figure 3.6a at the very least. To achieve this, the players must devote time together, in addition to simple everyday meetings, and be prepared mutually to give their best attention to the subtle details of their respective terms of reference and of their individual personalities.[2]

In the SDM project, the players found the minimal shared cultural envelope almost naturally and this allowed them to act quickly and coherently in the face of the fixed objectives. But the circumstances were such as to require prompt effort by everyone. For the longer term, an action such as the creation of the Group orientation committee, which brought together the sixty most senior executives with the chairman two or three times a year, contributed considerably to the establishment of a MSCE at the Rhône-Poulenc Group level. This did much to facilitate inter-sector relations and the necessary mobilization, when the stakes required it. This orientation committee worked on the Group values project and ratified the current statement of principles for action.

At another level, the regular and repeated briefings at Rhône-Poulenc Agro, which also allowed room for socializing, was a driving force in the development of a MSCE for Agro.

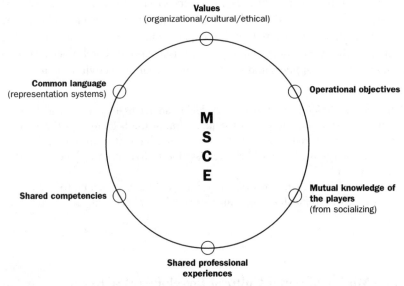

Figure 3.6a   *Minimal shared cultural envelope*

It is not sufficient to bring into play or to increase the tools of management and the new methods. These must be made consistent at the same time in the management systems and in the MSCE.

One of the great pitfalls of linear and controlling management is to increase the methods and tools that are imposed or indeed superimposed on the players, leading to their disempowerment through an exogenous approach. In fact, recourse to outside consultants often runs the risk of compounding this management pathology. It is therefore important for consultants called upon to provide one-off tools to respond with the request for managers to think about the alignment of the different logical levels of Figure 3.6a and thereby even invite the players to enter into a process of collective understanding organized around this MSCE.

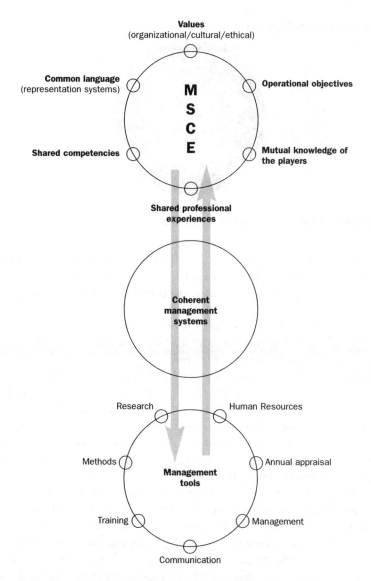

Figure 3.6b *Construction and alignment levels of shared visions*

In my personal experience, I can vouch for the federative power of EVC as a common management tool, and all observers have confirmed this.

The management questionnaire also fulfilled such a role, in my opinion more effectively than the appraisal system which hardly fulfils its federative role, despite its regular use going back almost ten years. Evaluating people is still a subjective and plural activity, apart from being theoretically federative, which goes to show that it is the use made of it that is the true value of a tool.

7 Collective intelligence

Figure 3.7a *Definition of collective intelligence*

Dynamic. By this we mean that collective intelligence is a process permanently in motion that cannot be stopped or shown in a frozen diagram. This gives rise to much frustration and unease that provoke resistance.

Players. It is advisable to bring people out of a logic of passive obedience, that is only active or reactive, and lead each member of the organization progressively into becoming proactive.

Co-responsibility. It is a long way from the process of liberation and promotion of personal rights to the logic of responsibility and free assimilation of stakes and duties. Victor Frankl, the great Viennese therapist, speaking to Americans, told them that there was a continent to be crossed. In the east of the USA, there was certainly the Statue of Liberty, but there was still the whole country to cross before building the statue of Responsibility in the west.

Interconnected. The players have to be joined to one another. They have to pass from being a collection of individuals to being a community via the stage of being an effective team motivated by a common spirit.

Soft. The change and harmony of the players' systems of representation. Do they speak the same language? Do they have the same 'cultural envelope', made up of objectives, values, skills, language, experience and sociability?

Hard. The alignment of management systems (recruitment, organization charts, pay scales, control and information systems, and so on), as well as the means of communication (such as electronic messaging for instance).

Alliance. We are thinking of the rational and irrational harmony between the parties who accept their differences and adhere to a relationship that allows their common path to be followed, despite contradictions, suffering and frustration.

Shared vision(s). This is the agreement on the aims and stakes that alone allows control of complex systems and lends meaning to the movement and the losses/failures at each stage of change.

If a frog is placed in a pan of boiling water it will struggle and may succeed in jumping out. But if one puts the same frog in a pan of cold water and heats it progressively in stages, this same frog may well be cooked without having moved.[3] Food for thought as much for large and small firms as for individual managers. How many businesses and bosses in France have lived through such an experience? We are thinking here of Noël Tichy's book, *Control Your Destiny or Someone Else Will*[4] that describes the saga of General Electric since 1981.

The logic of collective intelligence can alone enable the business to centre itself on the clients' needs, overcome the remoteness and weight of bureaucracy, and combat the arrogance or simply the obliviousness of executives who are often victims of the syndrome of success and cannot – like the frog – detect the faint signals that nevertheless reach them. Let us turn to Charles Handy's theory of the two curves:

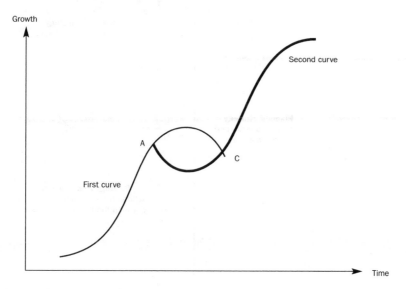

Figure 3.7b *The two curves of the business after Charles Handy*

When we arrive at point C on the first curve, the frog is already cooked. The implementation of collective intelligence that is a condition of permanent renewal should have been put in place at the beginning of the second curve, at point A.

8 Target logic, constructivist logic

The managers in the uncertainty of complexity can no longer be content to make plans. Paradoxically, their planning process runs the risk of abandoning the attitude of permanent watchfulness and sensitivity to faint signals. They must therefore ensure a delicate dynamic that consists in combining target

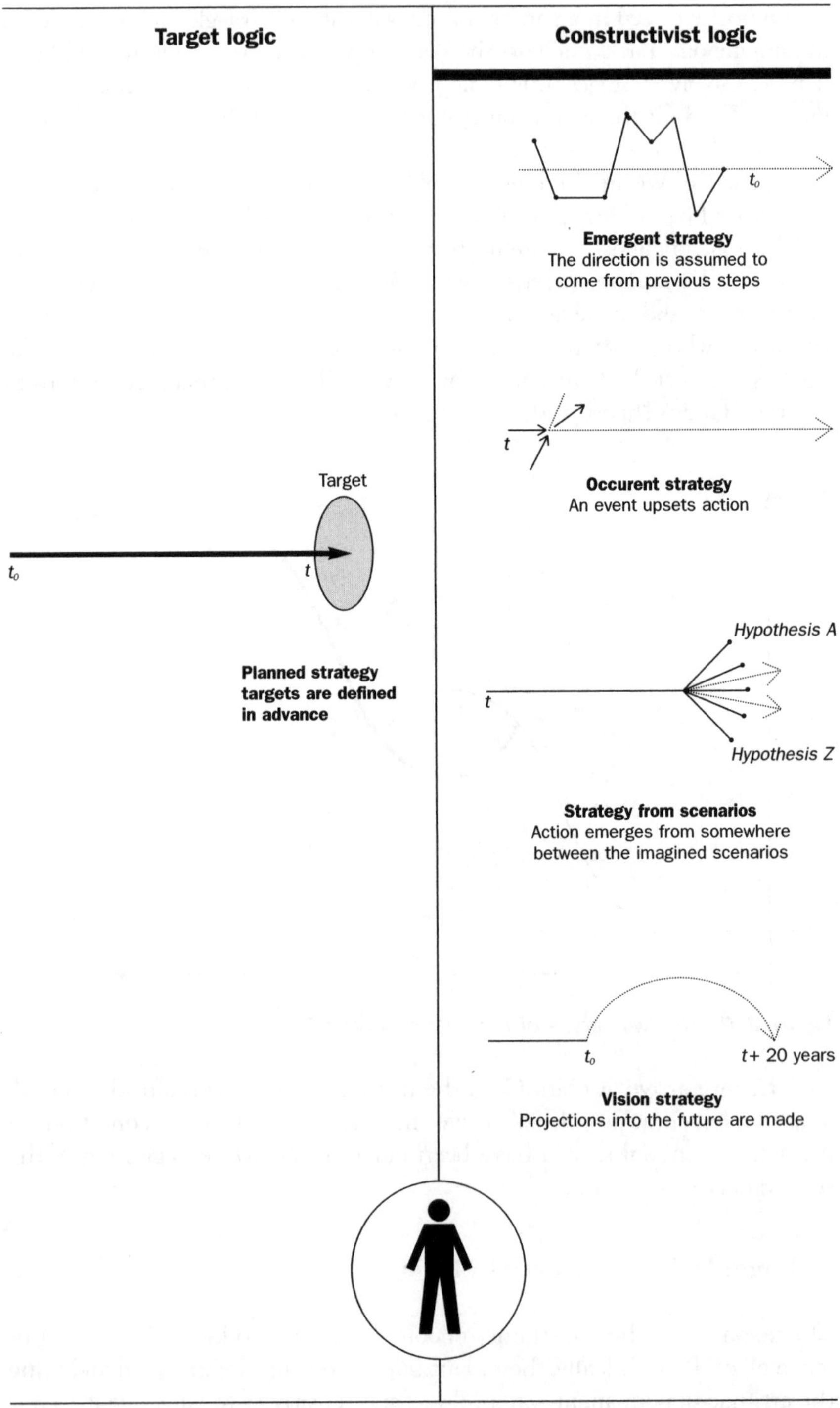

Target logic

Constructivist logic

Emergent strategy
The direction is assumed to
come from previous steps

t_o

Occurent strategy
An event upsets action

Target

t_o t

**Planned strategy
targets are defined
in advance**

Hypothesis A

t

Hypothesis Z

Strategy from scenarios
Action emerges from somewhere
between the imagined scenarios

t_o t+ 20 years

Vision strategy
Projections into the future are made

Figure 3.8a Strategic thinking between two approaches: target and constructivist

logic with constructivist logic, and by means of a trial and error approach be ready at any time to reconfigure their strategy by mobilizing the internal and external players involved. This dynamic is uncomfortable because it does not offer the security of foresight and certainty; it nevertheless becomes inescapable.

At the beginning of the 1990s, I was one of the chief players in the launch of two new products that were thought to be very promising.

The first – a fungicide for cereals – was launched according to a plan that was imposed by the executive committee (to which I belonged), at the time when the organization was very centralized. We had been incapable of hearing the signals that our internal researchers and our future customers were sending us. The launch plan (date, objectives, price) was imposed and followed whatever the cost. The product was a failure; it is slowly being redeveloped after losing several years of life.

The second – our insecticide Fipronil (see below) – was placed on the different markets in a much more targeted way, taking account of the requirements of each segment and of the signals received along the way. It benefited from the new approach to the definition of objectives (commitments, hopes, dreams) that allowed room for innovation, creativity and permanent adaptation.

Four years later, this product is a great success for the company.

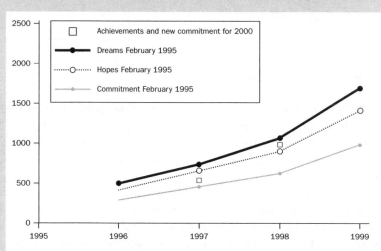

Figure 3.8b   *Illustration of the method: commitments – hopes – dreams (sales of Fipronil in agricultural markets)*

Compared with February 1995, the financial results for Fipronil are practically at the level for 'hopes' and the new commitments for 2000 are greatly ahead of the 'dreams'.

What is *Fipronil?*

Fipronil is a new generation insecticide discovered by Rhône-Poulenc Agro in 1989 and launched in 1994 for a number of uses. Its main characteristic is to be effective in very weak doses with a new way of working. It therefore marks significant progress for the environment. Authorized in more than fifty countries, it is used in agricultural markets (rice, maize, wheat, tropical crops), in the veterinary field (fleas and ticks), in hygiene and industry (cockroaches, ants, termites) and in the fight against the great scourges (locusts and mosquitoes).

Having shown itself to be a great technical and commercial success, *Fipronil* represented in 1998 a turnover of more than FF2.5bn for Rhône-Poulenc. Since 1997 it has been manufactured in a purpose-built factory located in Saint-Aubin-les-Elbeuf that involved an investment of FF500m.

9 Vision as a dynamic process

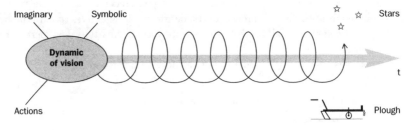

Figure 3.9 *The continuous dynamic of the vision*

The *symbolic* is the set of texts, documents and objective communications around the vision (brochures, videos, displays, and so on). In fact this only represents 20 per cent of the work that has to be done for the vision to be shared. However, the majority of managers believe that this symbolic material is enough.

The *imaginary* represents that which is built in terms of meaning in the consciousness of the players. It is the most important work to be done and represents 80 per cent of the energy to be expended.

The *action*, through concrete implementation on the ground, consists of enabling the players, through verbal and non-verbal exchanges, to extract by a common action all that is implicit in the definition of a common project. Concrete realization of projects allows one to move on to the explicit.

It is a question of combining these three vectors into a 'loop' process where, like the farm-worker ploughing his furrow while watching the stars, the manager combines the short term with the long term.

People are forever talking about the global vision of the company. In fact, for the majority of the players, what they work with is the adaptation of this vision to their 'unity of membership'. Being closely connected to the markets, these local decentralized visions, part of the total global vision, are permanently evolving while remaining consistent with the whole.

Making the global vision evolve is more difficult and cannot be done so often, because large liners are not as easy to steer as sailing boats.

For example, in our profession it is essential nowadays to pay more attention than was done a few years ago to the impact of plant biotechnologies on agriculture. But how do we express and integrate this in the vision and then in reality? This requires lengthy reflection before expressing a willingness that truly involves the company, after the stakes have been thoroughly understood and shared by all.

10 From monologic to teleologic

Monologic. The only existing logic, excluding any other.

Dialogic. Term created by Edgar Morin, corresponding to the coexistence of two logics of different nature and order, each having its own life.

Teleologic (from the Greek *Telos*: purpose). A logic centred on the overall purpose.

One of the main pitfalls for management lies in believing that one has performed the act of communication because one has published and 'communicated' notices or put them on display. A vision does not take on meaning for players unless they have made sense of it in their minds, and will only be shared if they have experienced the feeling of being able to express them, be listened to and considered. There is no co-responsibility without a minimum of equality.

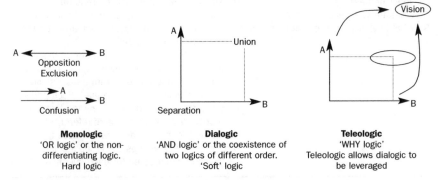

Source: After Dominique Genelot in *Manager dans la Complexité* and Jacques Fauvet and Jean-René Fourtou in *La Passion d'Entreprendre*, op.cit.

Figure 3.10 *The vision allows dialogics to be transcended and leveraged*

I discovered the word teleologic when I read the book by J.-R. Fourtou, *La Passion d'Entreprendre*, after he first joined the Rhône-Poulenc Group. I did not commit the concept to memory as it seemed too theoretical. More than the words, what seems to me most important today is to move from the logic of 'or' to the logic of 'and'; this is very urgent for all business people. Too many managers are lagging in this approach. Signing up the actions of everyone in a mission with an end that is known and shared by all enables greater effectiveness to be achieved. Many in the teams are convinced without necessarily knowing that teleologic is involved, because in reality the man of action has too little time to theorize.

11 A practical method for building a shared vision

A group of less than ten can use this method to build its vision in a minimum of half a day. The members of the team may have prepared the questions in advance, but this is not essential. The fact of having to prepare them in the room requires each of the participants to frame the five questions clearly.

Content	Process
Five questions	*Six stages*
1. How do you see your company in five years?	**1.** PIR (Prior Individual Reflection). The individual participants reply by filling in *Post-it* slips that are fastened to a paperboard.
2. How do you see your company in one year?	**2.** Each person reads out his or her answers to the five questions.
3. What are your main internal and external stakes? (If there is time, one can discuss Strengths/weaknesses, Threats/opportunities)	**3.** Each person listens to the others with no discussion. Only questions for clarification are allowed.
4. What are your recommendations?	**4.** METACOMMUNICATION. There is no discussion of content once everyone has read out his or her replies, but views on the process are exchanged. This is the stage that is most often missing in the 'sharing of representations', but which transforms the process from a discussion into a 'dialogue' or 'multilogue'. Each person takes the time and the means to identify and respect the other's frame of reference*.
5. What is your personal contribution?	**5.** The first four questions are discussed.
	6. Using the *Post-it* slips the group's collective vision is constructed for each question.

* I refer the reader to the simple and basic example of Bohring's drawing (now well known) in which one can see a young woman and at the same time in the same drawing an old woman. One has to see the young woman *and* the old woman.

Figure 3.11a *Method for developing a vision as a group*

The first four questions put the participants in the position of senior executives – become vizier instead of the vizier – thus allowing them to talk responsibly about the stakes and take an overall view. The fifth question puts them back in their own job.

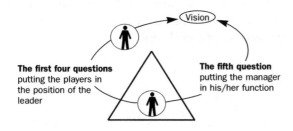

The first four questions
putting the players in
the position of the
leader

The fifth question
putting the manager
in his/her function

Figure 3.11b *Building a shared vision*

This method which we have tried more than a hundred times is not completely adequate to build a very precise vision. It does however allow the following to be achieved with remarkable effect:

1. *A collective vision is created*, formalized through the use of *Post-it* slips, in a very short time, and even using a team that is new or relatively in conflict and has never practised team building.
2. *Players are motivated on an equal footing.* The leader expresses his or her views like the others and sees to it that he/she never speaks first or last. Ideally, he/she should be the penultimate speaker. The other members of the team deliver their responses to the five questions while standing, something that, in the majority of cases, none has encountered before in such a context. They also have the opportunity to develop their delivery in a way that is stimulating and empowering.
3. *It allows the move from agreement/disagreement to agreement/disagreement/ misunderstanding* where agreement is much more important than misunderstanding and disagreement (Figure 3.11c). This normally comes as a pleasant surprise for the team members.

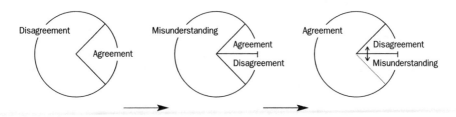

Figure 3.11c *Change in a group's representation of reality*

4. *It provides an immediate first experience of effective teamwork for a group that is still only at the stage of a collection of individuals*, irrespective of any formulation of a shared vision.

5. *It creates a break from routine* for a team whose players belong to a technical or operational culture. This approach makes them receptive to the concept of process and meaning and initiates them in metacommunication – communicating about communication – an absolutely essential approach to the management of complexity.

The Evolution of Teams

12 Six-stage model

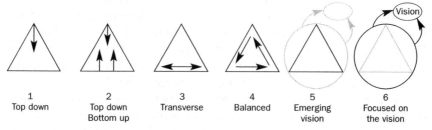

Figure 3.12a *Model in six stages*

This model in six stages, rather like the steps of a staircase, shows in an over-simplified but operational way the team's stages of development. It provides self-diagnostics for the team and allows the consultant to define the nature of the appropriate input for team building.

Though presented here in linear form, and therefore very scaled down, it is in fact 'holomorphic' like almost all the other models examined here. The diagnostic ought to be presented as a histogram in which each stage would correspond to a column, a team being obviously engaged in the six modes or stages at the same time.

We should here explain several basic concepts.[5] Each stage is necessary and is related to a development stage to which corresponds a positioning of the players and a specific problem.

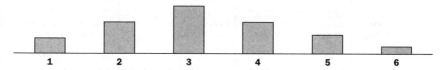

Figure 3.12b *The six stages shown as a histogram*

1. The creation phase for the team.
2. The stage where the head must collect people together and function like a star and decide and arbitrate.
3. The stage where transverse and decompartmentalized functioning must prevail and the head be partially absent and where delegation or preferably empowerment exists.
4. The stage where finally decisions are taken as a group even though the hierarchical role remains predominant.
5. As the common vision emerges, circular functioning, equality of the players, is progressively established.

6. The vision(s) being shared or, at least, the stakes taken on board by all, co-responsibility prevails and the hierarchical role becomes secondary, even mainly formal (for purely practical or institutional reasons).

This model makes it incumbent upon the managers, while duly recognizing the importance of the set of problems (advantages and pitfalls) to be able to provide at each stage, in a 'situational management'[6] logic, the functioning configuration that suits the players, the problems, the situation and its contradictions. It is not evident that this will be the case, because the organizational culture and the development stage of the players may prevent it. Consider, for example, a director who dares not give proof of authority and dares not go through stages 1 and 2, or contrastingly one who loses his ontological security if he loses the external indicators of his status (the lobster complex[7]) at stages 5 and 6.

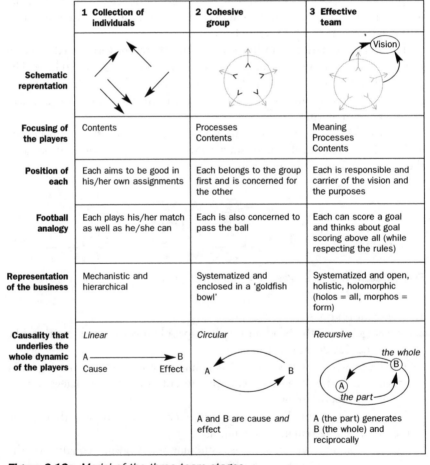

Figure 3.12c *Model of the three team stages*

Progression from stage 1 to stage 6 can be achieved in a single session, especially, for example, using the vision development shown above. However, the building of an identification and an understanding at the heart of the group which will allow it to change register at will implies months of work, a head capable of living through such a situation and who is a gifted teacher, and if necessary an accompanying process by an external change agent.

One should be aware of the 'freezer effect'. Embarking on stage 1 or 2 towards stages 4 and 5, that decision, when announced and implemented by the head and the members of the team, may disclose a snag that unfortunately often occurs. It can imply a step backwards due to an existing crisis situation, or hasty, unconcerted and impulsive decisions by the head, who has only initiated a cosmetic change of behaviour (type 1 change: only exterior behaviour changes) and who has not altered his profound attitude (type 2 change involving beliefs and representation systems). This backward step cancels at a stroke all the work done previously and destroys the credibility of the head's action and words. This is what we call the freezer effect. Products can be defrosted once, but not twice. All the more so with human beings.

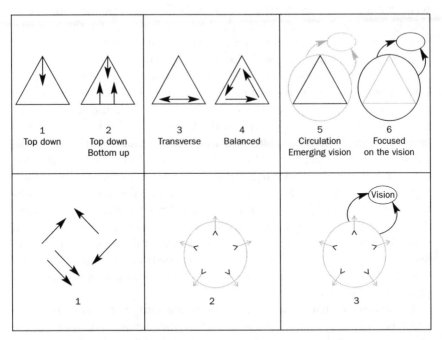

Figure 3.12d *Correspondence between Figures 3.12a and 3.12c*

All the comments in Figure 3.12a apply equally to Figure 3.12c. We shall now examine each element of Figure 3.12c.

1. A schematic representation

The three stages function like a system of communicating vessels, but unfortunately only too often the valves between them may close. If the 'collection of individuals' is the stage where all managers develop their 'talent' and try to become the best professionals in their domain, excellent! However, the result is often territorial struggles and 'baronies'.

The 'cohesive group' is the one in which the transverse dynamic is alive (cross-functionality, Drucker's 'T-men', and so on), and where the players live permanently on 'dialogics', each knowing that taking into account the other's framework of reference is necessary before a decision and that a good decision is not only the 'technical' decision but the 'co-developed' decision (in order to avoid the classic disempowering syndromes of imposed solutions: 'Not Invented Here'). We note that in identity terms, the 'individual', a 'team member' in the first stage, becomes a 'person', that is a 'relational being'. The danger for this group, however, may be that of a united group, internally cohesive, but which, being closed in on itself, may become a 'chapel', an exclusive club, even a Mafia team, competitive and looking after its own interests, or simply perceived as such despite its good and sincere intentions.

We have seen management teams that, after some very positive work on team building, have been regarded as focused on themselves and insufficiently communicative even though they were working for the common good of all. The same goes for certain company entities that are regarded as 'Celtic villages' by the 'Romans' who surround them.

Once the membership, everyone's contribution and the aims have been verified, the 'effective team' will turn the order levels upside down and will experience the identities in the opposite way through the stages of the growth process. In the growth process, the first requirement is to exist and to know who one is. It is only after this that one will truly be able to belong, feel competent and recognized by others as such and so actually co-develop common solutions, abandoning personal 'blocks' (wanting to 'be right'), expressing one's fears and needs and taking responsibility for one's own self-image and identity. William Schutz,[8] the celebrated American consultant, describes this very well through the concepts of inclusion (membership), control or influence (each person's contribution to the group's output and his/her own position so far as power is concerned) and openness/frankness (the ability to show that one is sincere, transparent and close by sharing one's preferences and needs).

It seems to us that in an effective team one further step must be taken which is a major qualitative leap and a real identity change. The ability of the players to surpass themselves – even to give priority not only to otherness as in the preceding stages but to the sense of the 'common good', a kind of sense to serve, say a capacity for giving of oneself that extends beyond a relationship to another while still including it – this ability is something that could be described as a form of 'offering' and 'communion'. The representation of the relationship with others is seen as a system open to others and to the environment and illuminated by the values that are built on this same relationship. This is visible in companies. Mr So-and-So works for himself or for his boss, or for the common good of the company, even the company that cares about its environment. This brings us to the whole question of the representation of the company and of the person in his environment, in particular concerning the concept of value creation. Are we talking about value for the shareholder or value for all the participants (stakeholders), such as clients, staff, suppliers, people in the environment?

The danger for this stage is that which is common to all manipulation or twisting of meaning. For example, speeches about values that are not translated into facts, the fashion of ethics justifiably attacked by some,[9] paternalistic declarations that are sometimes cynically exploitative, and so on.

Making teams progress has always been one of my concerns. From the beginning of the 1980s, I had initiated seminars on team functioning using business games.

Then, around 1984–85, for a year I arranged for my executive committee meetings to be videoed. The recordings were then analysed and criticized by the group with a consultant. It has nevertheless remained for me a means of showing what should or should not be done, rather than a theoretical knowledge of concepts.

At the beginning of the 1990s, the participation of Vincent Lenhardt at a multicultural executive committee meeting had the same objective. He was a critical observer who could reserve his judgement before making decisive contributions to the progress of the group.

There were some memorable moments, out of the ordinary for all, at this gathering, such as the welcoming of new members to the team, an agenda item that is generally allocated too little time, but which can in fact save time and add to the efficiency of the group.

The energy required of a leader in order to sustain the performance level of a team is enormous. Generally, one blows oneself up in this task and very often some energy breakdowns happen after a while.

2. What is an effective team?

It is of course a team that wins. However, this phrase contains a number of ambiguities. Does the end justify the means? What values are taken into account? Does the group take priority over the individual? And where are the boundaries? Without wishing to embark on a lengthy philosophical and anthropological debate, we will put forward two views.

On the one hand, we will go along with Will Schutz and say that if a team fails, it is most frequently because one or more of its members are rigid (rigid persons are those who see the representation of themselves threatened), and not only because there are disagreements, no common goals, the approach to solving problems varies between members, or because sensitivities are not integrated. Schutz has his own way of expressing what we describe as the 'lobster complex'. We will take the explanation further and say that in our experience as a consultant and psychotherapist, a group becomes cohesive only when its members recognize themselves to be human beings who accept their weak points, their injuries even, and who can talk about them to themselves and to others. A crowd becomes a 'collectivity' when its members feel that they belong to some kind of entity, whether institutional or factual (reacting together to an external threat). This collectivity becomes a 'community' when its members accept and are prepared to take everyone's injury into account, even that of the weakest.[10] This is when the members of this team develop, from the individuals, then the persons (relation beings) that they were and still are, into 'communion beings'. They accept each other truly as 'beings' and together live through this adherence to 'the being'.[11]

On the other hand, we feel it useful to state that for us the effective team is the one that includes not only cohesive persons, but persons who build an entity that is a carrier of meaning, with values and aims that are carriers of meaning. They are beings of communion who, while they accept that they are ephemeral, act in the name of a kind of transcendence. In other words, while accepting themselves with modesty, they commit themselves with conviction to serving strong values. This transcendence, if it illuminates action, may be subjective and be the object of all deviations. However, if it inspires action and make it a 'just' act, while respecting the trilogy of truth, justice and conscience, and integrating within it respect for the other person[12] (which most often presupposes a combination of discernment and courage), it will allow the jointly responsible members of a team to propose winning deeds, even if there is the prospect of failure. The anthropology thus developed in the effective business teams may lead to the building of *homo patiens*[13] persons, though there is no certainty that this will be achieved. Those who possess sufficient ontological security have the courage to take risks, sometimes put their head on the block and make actions that are carriers of meaning, whatever the cost to them, because they take responsibility for all the consequences. To quote Eric Berne and his remark on the winner: 'He is the one who knows what he will do if he loses'.

3. The players' positioning in their commitment

Moving from content to process does not do away with the former. But in the case of stage 2, the process takes the first place and the content is not 'added'; it is recorded in a 'higher order' that 'accomplishes' it without abolishing it. For example, if, as a controller, instead of developing a scheme on my own like an expert and imposing it as the right technical solution, I consult the people involved, ask them what they need, listen to their suggestions, I am then functioning in a process of co-development that takes first place and will endow the system finally established – the content – with a quality of a different nature. I will probably have integrated parameters that I would have missed, and the users concerned will probably have more readily endorsed the chosen solutions.

In the third stage, if the vision is shared, the meaning that it represents comes first, and the processes that will flow from it, then the contents, will be recorded in a hierarchy. The processes and contents will not be abolished but on the contrary magnified. It is paramount for the players of change first of all to answer the questions: 'Why?' and 'For what?', or 'What is it about?', 'What is at stake?' then 'How?' and finally simply 'Well, what do we do?'.

1. Questions on meaning (vision, strategy)	What are the stakes? What is it about? Why have we reached this point? What are our aims? What is important? What is urgent?
2. Questions on processes	How should we set about it? What method do we adopt? What are the roles? Who decides? How do we link together?
3. Question on content	What are we doing? What are we deciding? Where, when and who does what?

Figure 3.12e *Hierarchy of meaning, processes and contents*

For a long time I have been convinced that the strength of a team is not necessarily proportional to the sum of the individual qualities of its members. If these qualities are not put to the service of a shared objective, we witness some striking individual feats, but these may not necessarily serve the common interest.

One of my colleagues in the Rhône-Poulenc Human Resources Department – a great authority on the Group and its staff – who recently retired, told me at his departure that what struck him from observing the Agro teams all over the world was that they were among the most effective in the Group, albeit that they generally consisted of the 'good' and the 'average' rather than the 'cream'.

This was a compliment for the management. J.-R. Fourtou, who is from the South West of France, often chooses the example of rugby to defend his convictions about team spirit. France's victory in the Football World Cup is another example of a team capable of exceeding itself, where we see in a crucial match a back whose first role is not goal scoring yet nonetheless secures the two decisive goals necessary for the group to win.

Though developed over a quite a short period, the SDM operation was no doubt lived through– keeping things in proportion – like a World Cup type of event, where the tension and galvanization of their spirits enable the individuals and the teams that they make up surpass themselves, fulfil themselves and ultimately act in the service of an objective truly shared and understood by all.

The whole problem subsequently, after such a period of tension and achievement, is maintaining the same level of performance. This requires permanent attention and effort and generally one is only partially successful in this.

4. The analogy of football

France's victory in the Football World Cup is a fine metaphor for what a business team functioning as a collective intelligence can experience. One can speak of an effective team for France, a team that wins. A film produced by the French television network Canal +, *Les Bleus dans les Yeux*, is especially revealing as to how concentration, and focusing on aims and the complex processes, come first as compared with the spectacular and decisive moments of the matches. It would take too much space to analyse here all the parameters of this event that stretched over several weeks. We would simply note that:

- Each player must be at the top of his form (stage 1);
- He has the constant feeling of joint responsibility (stage 2) and must always pass or receive the ball;
- He is focused on the objective: sees to it that someone in the team scores a goal; he is 'carrier of everything', for a back may sometimes mark more than one forward, but not at any price: he must respect the rules, otherwise he risks getting the red card;
- Each player is carrier of a planned strategy that is at the same time emergent, occurrent and permanently reconfigured, in a wonderful process of self-organization where each person's skill is optimized before the skill of everyone and of the situation, a marvellous example of management in complexity. There is no organization chart in a football team!
- Finally, more than ever the role of the coach, his personality (humility, tenacity, confidence in unsettling situations, reliability, simplicity, rigour, support, excellence) and in particular his role of accompanist show the extent to which the agent of change, who does not act himself (he is not

the operator who scores the goals) but knows how to accompany the players, determines the collective success, serving as a model for the managers of today and tomorrow.

5. Representation of the business and types of causality

For the business to function as a collective intelligence, as an effective team in fact, it is absolutely fundamental for the representations held by the players in the business to transfer from the mechanical to the systemic model (relatively self-contained), then to the open and holomorphic systemic model. The stumbling block proclaimed by all companies that wish to experience this new management of complexity arises from the fact that the change in structures, strategies and systems cannot be completed if the managers do not acquire not only new behaviours but also a new identity and new representation systems.

Sumantra Goshal and Christopher Bartlett[14] have shown this magnificently in their analysis of the mutations of General Electric, ABB and other examples of change. They recall this sentence of a manager complaining that 'we tried to implement third generation strategies, in second generation companies led by first generation managers'. By this we mean innovation strategies that were not only technological, but leading to the creation of service relations rather than products (third generation), and end up with new approaches to business with companies organized as inverse pyramids but not yet networked (second generation), and managers left as engineers in the production logics (first generation).

This representation can only change if the players have truly integrated into the facts the concepts of causality that correspond to these three stages and notably the principle of 'recursion'.

A is no longer only the cause or the effect opposite B. A has become cause and effect opposite B, and A, the part, generates B, which is the whole, and in turn is generated by B. The person is in the business and builds it, and the business is in the person and builds him. The project team ensures, through an apparently limited participation, in terms of turnover for example, the success of the business, and the business must ensure the success of its project group. This dynamic is something more than reciprocity, because it contains mutual inclusion and interdependence of identity, which is the only condition for success of the two poles A and B.

If we take the analogy of the human body, a body cell may nourish, cure or infect the whole body, and inversely the body (the other cells and the organization of everything which is greater than the sum of its parts) may nourish, cure or infect the cell. Hence the importance of 'detail' in the theory of complexity. This holomorphic dimension, in which each manager or each team is a hologram of the whole of the business, exists in space and time. The approach of this new management consists precisely in the coherence of the proposed actions.

- *In time.* We can see the extent to which a missed interview, a badly conducted meeting or a single unnecessarily authoritarian decision, a contradiction with the decisions of previous actions, may cancel a whole range of predispositions, and especially confidence. Our experience as consultant and guide to change has caused us on many occasions to warn executives against actions or one-shot seminars that were supposed to solve a problem or float an idea. We see to it that they are mindful of the necessity of subscribing this will to change in a vision creating global coherence in time, in order to allow the players to make the necessary advancement to take on board the stakes, solutions and decisions (by experiencing their grief, assimilation of the stakes, co-development of decisions, and so on).
- *In space.* J.C. Collins and J.I. Porras[15] have shown this superbly in their study of companies with more 50 000 employees and more than fifty years old, being benchmarks of their professions, and therefore established without the need of the short-lived fashions of management. What constitutes the strength and the fruitfulness of these companies is the fact that each element of the company is a carrier of the vision and its genetic code. The company continually renews itself, while remaining faithful to its core values and there is no need for a rebellion in a Celtic village against the Roman occupiers in order to innovate or do one's job. Each entity is careful to set off on the right path: the executive team is 'in' each project group, and each project group is 'in' the executive team.

13 Managerial applications

We will now examine some applications of this management principle that is so difficult to implement: evaluation interview, recruitment, training, project group, meeting styles, and so on.

This table (Figure 3.13), presented in linear form, should be understood as aiming to ensure that the integrated stage 3 exceeds and completes the two previous stages.

We could add to the examples of implementing these representation systems:

- Conducting meetings, and especially managing the variable-geometry system of executive teams. How are they structured?
- Evidence shows that an organization chart runs the risk of freezing the players in a mechanical representation of the company. Instead stage 2 will contain processes or matrix systems (cf. the famous ABB matrix which, incidentally, has recently been called into question by Goran Lindahl). Finally, in the third stage, we talk about sharing the stakes and work on the overlapping of complex processes while carefully avoiding being too precise; this is linked to the way of co-developing objectives and not imposing them.

	Stage 1	Stage 2	Stage 3
Strategy	Planned and decided hierarchically.	Co-developed by the members of a united team.	Permanently reconfigured in a constructive and learning logic. A system open to external partnerships
Recruitment	Carried out by the manager who chooses the best internal or external professional.	By a process prepared, implemented and followed by the team integrating the technical, relational and complementary parameters.	First concern to see to it that the person is carrier of the appropriate vision for the company: between conformity or necessary rupture.
Evaluation interview	The hierarchical superior evaluates the subordinate placing him or herself outside the goldfish bowl: *A* evaluates *B*.	*A* evaluates *B* but after asking *B* to evaluate A (have I been a good boss?) as well as their relationship. *A* and *B* are in the bowl (evaluation of *A* by the subordinates or 360°).	*A* evaluates *B* but both will try to measure to what extent *B* has become carrier of the vision and the values.
Project groups	A senior executive recruits the participants, gives them procedures, the specifications, the means, a timetable and nominates a leader.	The executive becomes person of resources, invites the team to develop their procedures and accompanies them by being a guide to the process and not the content.	The executive: 1. insists on the contribution to the vision of the company that represents the project; 2. sees to it that the executive team appoints itself as resources team to support the project. 3. transforms the Roman environment into a Celtic environment (works for a cultural change of the structure).
Training for change	Focused on *contents*. Conceived with the development of tools of excellence (courses, catalogues, information centres, etc.)	Conceived through *processes*. Training action integrating the life of the organization and on the other hand the personal projects of the players (career plans and bridges).	Focused on the *meaning*. Conceived as the strategic lever for implementing the vision. Carried by the directors and focused on the learning processes and the target skills to be acquired.

Figure 3.13 *Application of the previous representations and causality types (3 stages) to managerial situations*

- So far as collaboration with a consultant is concerned, these three steps may apply:
  1. The consultant provides a solution, expertise, advice, even – sometimes usefully – 'acts a replacement for...';
  2. The consultant sees to it that the group, or its client, co-develops or brings forth its solutions, while he still contributes his added value (experience, knowledge of other companies, management of the process – thus freeing the players who are too bound up with the contents and the stakes);
  3. The consultant, who is focused on the economic aims and/or the managerial values (depending on his personal skills), intervenes for greater coherence from the players with regard to the vision, for understanding the situation and for the degree of managerial development of the players. He will also intervene in an appropriate way on the meaning (importance, urgency, priority), the process (methods, linking and positioning of the players) and if required the contents (technical solutions, examples of best practice, and so on).

Throughout the whole period of the construction of SDM, the 'domain' working groups and the task forces were in fact project groups who worked outside the hierarchical systems. As I have said elsewhere, the accumulated tension and the sharing of the stakes, the requirement to move fast, the desire to succeed caused these groups to function at their highest performance level.

I was able to note the difference with the average level of performance of an executive committee type of group where it is rare to have topics that mobilize all of the members at the same time. Hence the various activities that one often sees: private conversations, reading or drafting correspondence, mobile telephone conversations.

It was this observation that led me to do away with the executive committee and to replace it with *ad hoc* committees relating to identified projects, involving people with a competency and/or a real interest in the subject under scrutiny. The executive committee was turned into a strategic committee that meets less frequently, but which tackles fundamental topics for which outside parties – clients, partners, consultants – are regularly invited. It now does its proper job.

The *ad hoc* groups worked on important subjects formerly handled by the executive committee. I could take part if I thought it necessary, but it was far from the rule. These groups have thus been able to develop their autonomy, including the taking of decisions on the allocation of significant resources.

To underline the transversality and informality, we had decided to dispense with an organization chart. The organization was represented by paving stones in relation to one another, and a document containing the 'yellow lines', the general rules for operation and the 'who does what', replaced the traditional organization chart (see diagram opposite).

The results of the social barometer showed that this more fluid organization, less structured but more mobile, did not prevent the staff from considering that their roles were better defined than before (71 per cent compared with 57 per cent). Apparently, there were in that organization many of the ingredients and components of the effective team.

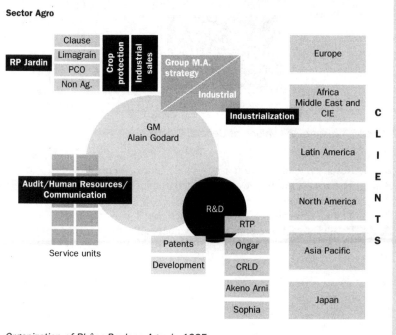

Organization of Rhône-Poulenc Agro in 1995

Concerning recruitment, some high level managers rejoined Rhône-Poulenc Agro precisely for this reason.

As I have stated elsewhere, maintaining such an approach is a drain on the leader's energy. There is a real risk that the effectiveness of some basic processes will be diluted, hence the need to return sometimes to the behaviours that belong to stage 2.

This principle is now adopted by the Rhône-Poulenc Group (see pp. 62 and 63) and is beginning to be put into practice. However, much effort is still required in the area of communication, training and practical demonstration of rule application in order for it to influence behaviour at the desired level.

The stress placed on values in the SDM operation enabled this approach to be relaunched at Group level. I supported the project from the Human Resources Department that was incidentally inspired by what had happened at General Electric (see diagram below illustrating the practice at General Electric). This approach consisted in placing each director and high-flyer on the double axis of delivering results against respecting values.

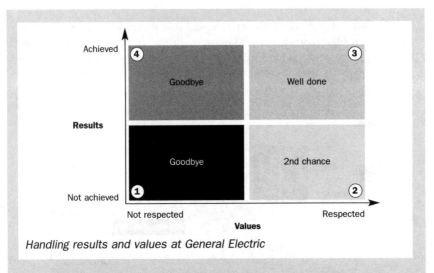

Handling results and values at General Electric

Box 1: Results and values are not respected: the person is sacked.
Box 2: The results are not respected but the values are: the person is given a second chance.
Box 3: Results and values are respected: well done!
Box 4: Results are achieved but not the values: collect your cards!

Managerial personality

Having thought about the management of teams, we will now turn to the personal dimension.

14 Subject/object ambiguity

How do we look at the managerial personality?

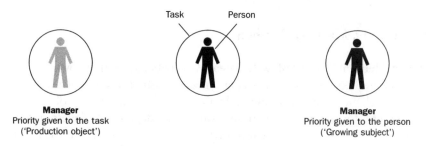

Figure 3.14 *The subject/object managerial ambiguity*

The managers in their job live in an inescapable ambiguity. They are at one and the same time 'growing subjects', unique persons and 'production objects', relatively replaceable. One does not exist without the other, and neither of the two poles can be reduced to the other. Nevertheless, the lasting quality of the company most frequently demands that a choice be made between these two poles. What psychological and moral contract does the company have in the face of its economic aims and its legal commitments? Must it guarantee employment or ensure employability? In other words, must it empower people with regard to their increase in competency and at the same time invite them to participate in a recursive activity (by themselves contributing to co-preserve the company they themselves sustain)?

It must be a permanent concern and guiding principle for managers to see to it that people are subjects and not objects. This is particularly true when one has to separate from a colleague. I have often had to do it and I have always striven to maintain the dignity of my colleagues by stressing the positive aspects of their personality, even though it was not suited to the needs of the company. Many have subsequently told me, after they have found stability in another post, that they have a positive memory of the interview.

I also pay particular attention to people seeking employment who come to me through personal or professional relational networks. Despite my heavy workload, I always try to find the time to have an 'essential' interview with such persons. Not because I have a job to offer them, which I do not generally have, but simply to make them feel that they exist, are not 'nothing' and must continue their search with hope and confidence.

I have several times received word from these persons a few months later. Now regarded, they tell me how useful this interview had been for them. These testimonials are one of the nicest presents one can receive and help one to be aware of what is important and essential.

15   Handy, Maslow, Herzberg

Handy, Herzberg and Maslow have each contributed in their own way to differentiate between the meaning and needs satisfied through work. These different elements are not mutually exclusive but are the evolutionary parameters for people, depending on their degree of development, concerning their needs and their motivations. It is important to have a look at the person who may welcome these different levels, and not be reductionist.

From these two opposing beliefs flow all management systems. In my opinion human beings have the two polarities in them potentially, and more or less unequally developed, and the managerial conditioning that surrounds them may have the greatest consequences.

I would be inclined to say that boring work is not natural for human beings, and therefore the situations in which someone works in this way must be controlled, unless one decides to change the nature of the work.

This is why I use the words 'pleasure' and 'game' so much in the company. Those men and women who can 'take pleasure' in the company do it naturally and, if one provides them with rules – which is not always the case – they are generally capable of self control.

A word of warning: without rules, this way of working known by the players can quickly degenerate. It therefore serves as an example to 'controllers' to show that nobody is capable of self-control.

I am therefore at heart in favour of theory **Y**, but I am not sufficiently naïve to believe that it can be applied in every case. One should be biased towards it whenever possible, because it is enriching both for the individual and for the company.

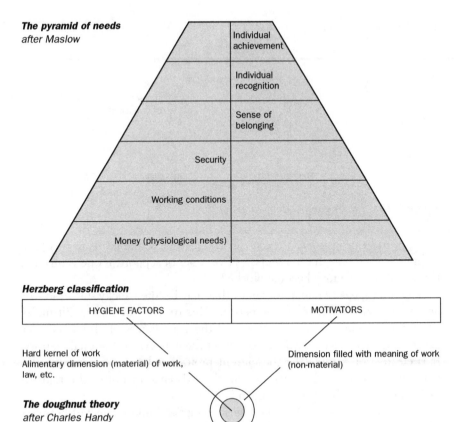

The pyramid of needs
after Maslow

	Individual achievement
	Individual recognition
	Sense of belonging
Security	
Working conditions	
Money (physiological needs)	

Herzberg classification

HYGIENE FACTORS	MOTIVATORS

Hard kernel of work
Alimentary dimension (material) of work, law, etc.

Dimension filled with meaning of work (non-material)

The doughnut theory
after Charles Handy

Figure 3.15a *Work, meaning and motivation*

	Theory X	**Theory Y**
Manager's belief concerning work	It is not natural to human being	It is natural to human being
Consequences so far as motivation is concerned	It must be exogenous Motivation must come from the outside	It can be endogenous The person is naturally motivated
Consequences so far as management is concerned	Must act to motivate Must control and sanction positively and negatively	Must create conditions where people will be able to express their motivation themselves. It is self-controlling and self-sanctioning
	exogenous dynamic →	*endogenous dynamic*

Figure 3.15b *McGregor's two theories: two different views of the managerial personality*

16   Trust

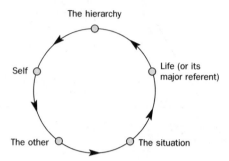

Figure 3.16a *The interdependent zones of trust*

Trust, confidence [L. *confidere*, con- sig. completeness, and *fidere*, to trust] is a complex conviction that presupposes five zones of support; if one is missing, the virtuous circle may become blocked.

When we speak of a major referent that may be 'life', 'lucky star', 'God' or any other major referent for the person. This trust is obviously built under the primary influence of education and the experiences of childhood, but also through the necessary development of the person's professional identity. It is clearly conditioned by the current professional environment and the managerial values of the organization: the existence or not of the right to make mistakes, right of initiative, and so on.

The establishment of a view of trust (reciprocal and recursive) between the players is a determining factor for the growth of co-players and the productiveness of every relational system. One sees it in the family, in teaching, in personal development and therapy, in the processes of apprenticeship, in spiritual accompaniment, in economic, political and social life. It is also the key to managerial life.

All the same, trusting is not a question of taking a naïve view of humanity, but may on the contrary be the result of an anthropology that accepts the ambiguity of the human beings, which is a condition of their free will, and integrates the attention paid to the positive part that one may believe present in every person.

Three zones are discernible in a person: the mask, the frog and the prince (or princess). The mask, a kind of social convention, does not always manage to hide the frog, that is, the injured and defensive part of every person. The latter shows itself, under stress, through defence mechanisms that have developed over time and through the more or less successful stages of the person's development. Unfortunately, these defences that have been the reason for recording and deciding to 'survive', often play a negative and blocking role in relations. It is important for the individuals facing one another to rediscover in the other the prince (or princess), who has remained intact and who may, through appropriate 're-decisions', replay a preponderant role. This is the aim of personal development and of psychotherapy in particular. But in business, trust is the attitude for which the hierarchical manager or the change agent are the main persons responsible. It results from this continually revived conviction that behind the mask and the frog, ever present and demanding vigilance and sympathy, there is a prince or a princess who may blossom and take control. It is the property of what is called the 'Pygmalion' effect, that is clearly identified in education and which enables the manager or the change agent to become a person of resources or a coach.

The alliance, which is something more than a simple relational contract since it is a reciprocal act of faith towards the other, will then be able to exist between the players, with reference to common values and a vision, while at the same time integrating tolerance, sometimes with frustration, pardon or compassion. The frogs and the masks sometimes remain too evident and too active for the taste of the players.

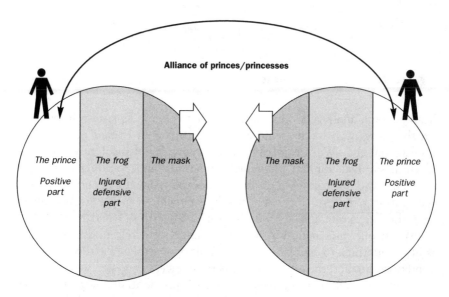

Figure 3.16b *The three layers of personality*

I cannot work or live without putting my trust in those around me. In the company, I have in the past had my doubts about some colleagues. My behaviour in this type of situation is widely known in the company, since I have often explained it quite openly. While my doubts remain unfounded, I try not to pay attention to them in my relations with the person, because I consider that we need to maintain trust between us in order to function and continue our search for the 'princes alliance'.

On the other hand, if on a fundamental matter my doubts hold sway and even if this situation is the result of a subjective feeling, I consider it necessary to say as much to the other person, which generally means that we have to part company.

For me, trust is never given out in percentages, it is given completely or not at all. This is why, when in the SDM process I sense the Group's confidence slipping away, I try to react quickly to re-establish it and thus maintain the relation.

17 Strokes

	Conditional	**Unconditional**
Positive	*Given for* *for external*	*Given for* *the person*
Negative	*acts or* *attributes*	*himself/* *herself*
Nil	*No sign of recognition*	

Figure 3.17a *The need for strokes*

Transactional analysis develops a theory that is too little known in business on the basic need for recognition for the person in his/her personal and professional life. We are talking about true psychological survival, even physical survival, for the individual, under the same heading as food or clothing. And one can learn to come out of the traumatic penury of signs of recognition (strokes), to avoid as much as possible negative strokes (albeit that they are preferable to the absence of any stroke) and to exchange positive strokes in a major way in order to create an environment of trust. It is also important to be able to give conditional strokes for the process of apprenticeship and the evaluation of performance.

A genuine training programme may enable people to discover where they are blocked in their 'economy' of strokes; some managers know how to give negative strokes but not positive ones. The usual remark one hears is: 'As the

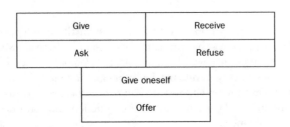

Figure 3.17b *The economy of strokes*

boss, if I see that the job is done well, I have nothing to say! But when things aren't going well, then I step in!' What do you think a team is going to do without any stroke? Rather than not have any conditional stroke (for what they have done well) or unconditional stroke (for the fact that they exist in the eyes of their boss, who would remind them of it from time to time, so signifying that they are important to him), they will try to find negative strokes by causing problems or creating situations of conflict. My reaction to such remarks is to underline the fact that it is precisely when everything is going well that it is important to say so, conditionally: 'Well done for your good results and your work' and unconditionally: 'It's good to work with you and have you in the team'. What might pass for flattery is on the contrary a way of maintaining good relations, provided it is sincere and not 'inflationary' of course and intended to establish a culture and relational beliefs in the style of the plentiful, the positive, the celebration of being together for work and pleasure. As the Americans say: one must have fun to be soft.

Some may give forth the positive but not the negative. They then accumulate the negative effects and one day there is an explosion. It is very important to be able to give conditional negative and not unconditional negative; every time that it is appropriate and not only at the annual appraisal interview; provided one sees to it that more of the positive is given often, thus making it easier for the negative to be accepted.

Others may not be able to receive strokes. This is very frustrating and often indicates a very rigid attitude in the people who not only find it hard to be close to their own feelings and to others, but feel that something is lacking and compensate for this by behaving as persecutors or saviours (by interfering with others in a disempowering way). Transactional analysis has much to say about this.[16]

Our experience of a large number of personnel development, training and team-building groups has shown us that very few managers have identified these needs clearly; even fewer have learnt how to handle them for themselves and for others. We have seen that it is possible in a relatively short time through explanations and a few suitable exercises to have a group achieving a major qualitative improvement by integrating this concept into its culture.

In our opinion it is an indispensable concept in building a managerial identity that aims to free itself from the lobster complex and acquire an ontological security (to be OK in the parlance of transactional analysis).

It is true that giving strokes in a clear and understandable way is not part of our education and our functioning system.

The Americans know how to do this much better than us, to the extent that their behaviour in this area sometimes makes us smile and we do not understand them.

Interestingly, the management questionnaire includes two questions on strokes given by the immediate superior:
– my immediate superior is able to say what things are going well;
– my immediate superior is able to say what things are not going well.

The results show that, on average, out of the 41 questions that make up the questionnaire, these two obtain the worst score, with particular mention of the incapacity of superiors to say what is going well.

The fact that this is discussed at the appraisal meeting provided for in the unfolding of the process has made everyone aware of this need to be recognized, that all people have, wherever they are.

In this context, the Orchid award, adapted from the 'American awards' by Rhône-Poulenc Agro, is today a tool and a bond that enables us to tell people things that are otherwise only too rarely stated. This is no doubt why it has fitted so well into the machinery of the company.

18 Levels of managerial identity

Not everyone can become a manager, but everyone can become a leader.

This model may be separated into three levels. The task for the advanced business is to make all the players if not managers, at least leaders. If we take the analogy of the cinema, the task is to make the actors (players) become, if possible, directors as well (move to the other side of the camera and learn how to manage people) and above all producers (that is, people concerned about the durability and growth of the company).

Professional or expert
– knows his profession
– knows how to do things

Manager
– knows how to achieve targets
– knows about management
– knows how to get people to do things

Leader
– knows how to define the targets
– knows the priorities and the aims
– knows what people can do

Figure 3.18 *Three levels of managerial identity*

There are still many engineers, that is, excellent professionals, in our large companies. The difference between manager and leader is perhaps not always understood, and I am not sure that people do not prefer to be recognized as managers rather than as leaders.

The managers generally have hierarchical power over the team, which is comfortable and reassuring.

The leaders have more of an influential role which they get from their experience and their behaviour; it is more difficult to have this recognized by others.

In modern organizations where projects are increasingly used, one can easily see that it is more difficult to find good candidates to lead projects, since the posts are less well recognized internally than those of hierarchical manager. This is one area where the revolution is not yet over.

19 Manager as order giver, manager as a resource, manager as carrier of meaning

In addition to the foregoing, we think that the stakes for advanced companies are even higher in transforming managers who give orders into managers of resources and ultimately into managers who are carriers of meaning.

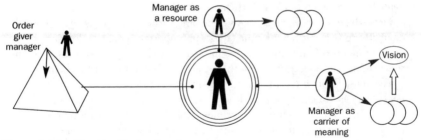

Figure 3.19a *The identity levels of managers*

What are managers who give orders?

They are people who, rightly, exert their role of deciders, controllers and hierarchical superiors, handing out protection and permission and defining the goals. At a certain stage they personify the meaning, but there is the danger that they will establish a dissymmetrical relation which invariably in the end threatens the growth of the other, and of the relation. The arbitrariness associated with the function culminates in establishing a 'symbiosis' where the parent/child relationship becomes dominant and prevents the adult/adult relationship. This leads to platitudes such as 'What time is it?' 'Whatever time you like, Mr President!'

What are the 'managers as a resource'?

They are people who first pay attention to the relation and to the process before taking up a stance with regard to the content. Before replying to a question, they first ask themselves whether it is for them or for the other to answer. They tend not to immerse themselves in the problems that are brought to them, but try to clarify the empowerment, to invite the partners to resolve their problem themselves by helping them to find their own solution. For this, they offer space, time, attention and support. They function more as trainers and facilitators. The Americans call them 'enablers', those who make the other capable. In complexity and the world of uncertainty, of the possible but only probable and never certain, the order givers run the risks of being trapped by their assurance, their expectations and their experience. Since reality does not conform to their expectations, they are in danger of wanting to make it bend to their will. But you cannot make plants grow by pulling on them. The persons of resources, on the other hand, go straight to the 'meta' position and retreat from it depending on what emerges; they therefore have more chance of helping others to act rather than acting in their place.

> For a long time I have felt myself to be a man of resources, even though my current supervisory role distances me from exercising this function in a conscious way. People in fact often express surprise that they are able to find me available to meet and talk with them.
>
> Nevertheless, I still meet many who are without resources, who I would characterize as never having time (these are important people!), forever talking on their mobile phones and reacting immediately to every event, thus justifying their lateness for meetings where their colleagues have to wait for them.
>
> To excuse them, it has to be recognized that being a person of resources is not necessarily an enviable position. It is a position where one has to accept ambiguities and frustrations that are sometimes difficult to bear. Taking time to listen to so and so's doubts and uncertainties when one has something else to do, or forcing oneself to pay attention to a moderately interesting presentation that has been laboriously prepared are important acts to 'support' another person, but they often turn out to be much less interesting than operational life.
>
> The persons of resources spend their time signalling to others that they are available. I believe that it is first of all necessary to be, and be seen to be, a person of resources, that is, available, before one can bring a 'meaning' to others; those who receive cannot receive from just anyone.
>
> In my opinion, this is the essential condition for finding oneself on some occasions a 'carrier of meaning' for others. I think I can say that this was what I was for my teams during the period of development and building of SDM.

What are the 'carriers of meaning'?

They are the persons who integrate the two previous stages but focus first on the stakes: external, internal, relational, identifying. They try to 'scratch where it itches' and do not rush at the contents or the processes. They are focused on the vision in the sense of the MSCE. They can personify the meaning for their colleagues who do not possess their level of consciousness and competence. There are decisions that must be taken alone. At such moments they can be the 'givers of meaning' but they will only have succeeded in their mission when they have made others capable of functioning without them, that is, by making others able to perceive the meaning of their action. They thus become 'welcomers' of meaning making others bring out the meaning progressively, not only because they see it externally (like stars whose light they see) but because they have it within them, uniquely and coming from their specific creativity and which means that each is definitely irreplaceable. The carriers of meaning are those who will generate the collective intelligence, that complex dynamic of inter-subjectivities which from now on will be broadening out and co-creative.

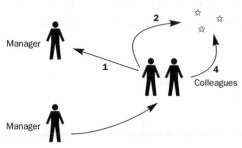

Figure 3.19b *The manager who is carrier of meaning*

Four phases describe the action of the managers who are carriers of the meaning:

1. They personify the meaning in the phase of healthy dependence, where their colleagues are at the beginning. They cannot yet see the stars and they use their manager as the star. The managers must guard against seeing themselves as stars, which is the trap of narcissism and the desire for power, a danger for all managers.
2. They enable the others to see the stars directly and objectively.
3. They position themselves as persons of resources to reflect back to the others their development of meaning and their building of meaning in their imagination.
4. They receive the meaning that comes from the construction through their colleagues and see to it that the community gives it credence and personifies it.

This complex role must adapt itself to each personality and each development and must obviously also take into account the degree of evolution of the team, and the nature of the problems and situations (their degree of urgency or importance).

This presupposes the skills of teacher and accompanist which are often attributed to the manager-coach.

20 Process of autonomy development

Being a key concept for the development of people and organizations, autonomy may be described as a sequence of stages, each made up of its own parameters: needs, pitfalls, positioning of the players.

The development of autonomy is based on a relational accompaniment where the accompanied entity (in the event a person, a team or an organization) forms part of a 'system' (including the entity that accompanies and the relation between the two).

Beyond the static stages (dependence, counterdependence, independence, interdependence) and the relational process, autonomy is a value. It is, as such, carrier of a meaning and an aim for the players. At stake there is still the building of a liberty that requires one to live through the paradoxes that this construction generates. One of the players helps the other to sort things out by him or herself.

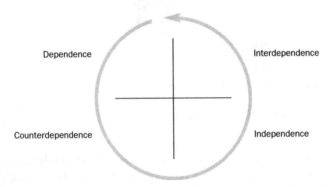

Figure 3.20a *Autonomy: the four stages*

Autonomy is more than independence (even though it is often implicitly restricted to this stage). It can also be represented like a dial to be traversed or a loop with its four successive stages and a process that is fortunately open and theoretically without end except for the limitations of the players: their potential for growth.

Figure 3.20b *Autonomy: a continuous process*

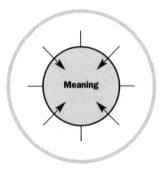

Figure 3.20c *Autonomy: its fifth stage*

At the heart of this dial or this loop one can inscribe a sort of metaposition, that of the meaning, personified by the shared vision(s) of the players. This sharing and interiorizing of the vision(s) by the players will enable them to be federated, even though they are located at different levels of autonomy.

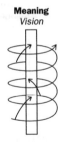

Figure 3.20d *Autonomy: centred and crossed by the meaning*

I believe that in order to develop, autonomy must be affirmed by the organization as one of its values. Empowerment is a good way of expressing it because no one is totally independent.

The EVC has been one of the factors in assuming autonomy by the players, by fixing in a simple way both the purpose (to create value to build the company of tomorrow) and an area where managers could operate without prior authorization. It was up to them to decide how to tackle their objective.

I have the feeling that those managers who have experienced a true autonomy will find it difficult to work under another system. In this sense, the principles that underpin SDM endow the operation with a durability that is felt and desired by the majority.

21 Levels of change

In systems theory one speaks of type 1 and type 2 changes. A type 1 change consists in doing something else but of the same nature, not 'doing the same thing'. For example, pressing further on the accelerator, making a greater effort, replacing one method with another, controlling behaviour. This can be very useful and effective. In therapy, one speaks of alcoholics who stop drinking, but who remain what are known as 'dry alcoholics'.

Most profound structure	Profound structure of persons	Attitudes	Managerial behaviours	Manager's environment
The prince still to be developed	Defence system and its injuries Their history, Their sub-conscious, Their emotions, Their body.	Beliefs Values	Management style Listening Communication Capacity for working in a group Protection/ permission Order giver Manager as a resource Carrier of meaning	Strategy Structures Systems
4	3	2	1	–1
	Internal (invisible)		**External (observable)**	

Figure 3.21a *The levels of change*

Type 2 change assumes that one is to go 'beneath the waterline of the iceberg', not press harder on the accelerator but change gear. It is in fact a question of changing the logic level. In their dreams, for example, people make all kinds of changes of activity – that is type 1. If they change to type 2, they wake up. The 'dry alcoholics' in a type 2 change carry out an analysis not only of their behaviour and change it, but go back to the causes, the suffering, the models, the decisions of the past that made of the choice of a decision the least bad decision, a solution paradoxically of survival, a palliative to suicide, to violence or to profound depression. Having identified their profound need, understood and perceived that they could handle it from now on directly and decide how to live, alcoholics can not only stop drinking but also stop being 'dry alcoholics' and live happily.

Business still seems to us to be full of these 'dry' order givers and controllers who are afflicted with the lobster complex. It is very important not to restrict oneself to simple changes of structure, strategy and system that we have called type 1 changes, as some top executives such as Jack Welch have understood after a number of years.

Alain Godard, by combining the work on the economics and the organization, insisted on a change in behaviour (type 1) but also on a change of values, beliefs and representation systems. He pushed the players to pursue the 'cultural revolution' (type 2) that was necessary for these players to be in a position to take on new and very complex forms of organization and management. I do not think that it is indispensable to have tackled a type 3 change for managers of businesses. But I think it is important for all individuals to have thought about this themselves, in their own fashion. One needs to have thought and talked about one's history, worked on one's emotions, bodily tensions and stress, identified one's psychological defences that often cut us off from the realities of others, identified the areas of insecurity and worked on one's fears in order not to be trapped by one's 'lobster shell' or one's 'frog skin'. Above all, one needs to have identified one's prince (type 4) and know it to be recognized by oneself and by enough other people who are competent and not complacent. All of this is extremely fruitful work.

Though the type 3 approach does not figure in the domain of the business, since it must remain a personal process, as part of the practice of the coach's profession I think it is desirable and certainly in my firm it is a prerequisite. As trainers of consultants with the Transformance team, for training courses entitled 'Coach and Teambuilding' based on twenty-two days in a year, we insist on this type 3 work as a prerequisite for the training. In our opinion, it is necessary for coach consultants to have cleaned their glasses on the inside if they wish others to do the same. They owe it to themselves not to be alone or the victim of their projections and impulses. Deontologically, they are required to go through such a course themselves and provide themselves with a permanent link of supervision and control.[17]

Being surrounded by people who criticize them too rarely to their face, executives no longer see their own defects and weaknesses. But in my view knowing one's strengths, weaknesses and limitations is essential. That is why on my own initiative I very quickly made the effort to get to know myself better, by taking a self awareness course, which was certainly more useful at the age of thirty (when I took the course) than at fifty. I can say from my own experience of management that one can change. My behaviour with regard to decentralization and empowerment, for example, changed profoundly within a few years.

I can see myself again at the end of the 1980s, as a manager insisting on cuts in the fixed unit costs on the basis of theoretical ratios, and imposing these without discussion with the operational staff, irrespective of the individual specific situations. I was simply adhering to the system of values that was in force at the time which I put up with.

It was through becoming aware of the limitations of this type of approach that I at first unconsciously, then more consciously, altered my system of values and developed behaviours that took more account of others. This does not prevent one at certain times from taking the most appropriate decision overall, after listening to, weighing and comparing the different solutions.

22 Grief

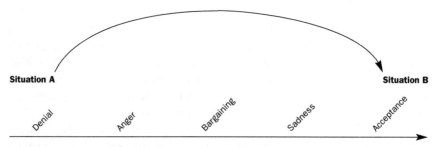

Figure 3.22 *The process of change and the stages of grief*

So far as the five stages of grief are concerned, the diagram in Figure 3.22a being inspired by the work of Elizabeth Kübler-Ross, here again we have a surprisingly little known concept to managers of change. It is important to identify for oneself the rhythms in the stages of grief. Everyone can build his own histogram of these five effects. Some people remain for long without seeing them, others move immediately to anger; still others only experience sadness, but for a long time.

The model is valid for collective change as well as for individual changes. It is valuable to know that these changes consume huge amounts of affects and that their metabolization by the players presupposes time, attention and the accompaniment from the managers themselves. Sometimes, despite their good faith, they are inadequate in this, because of their lack of time and resources, but also because of their status. Hence the importance, both for those that they accompany and for themselves, of external accompanists who are more neutral in relation to the stakes and skilled about the identifying and psychological processes of the different levels of change.

Finally, going through the stages is not sufficient. The act of giving them a meaning by explaining clearly the aims and sense of this change is a powerful factor for acceptance by the players of a difficult path. Giving notice of 'blood and tears', as Winston Churchill did in his time, is sometimes accepted more courageously when one knows 'why' and there is a celebration awaiting us at the end of our journey. This constitutes the whole dynamic of the mobilizing project and the 'shared vision' of the company.

With regard to the theory of grief and its different phases, which I already knew about, the SDM operation unfolded in a rather special way. The grief phase certainly occurred, through numerous leaflets from the unions seeking to devalue the approach and show that it was inappropriate.

Anger took over with the petition and the demand to participate in the meeting at Chazay in October. This phase grew to a scale that led me to face up to this anger directly by meeting all the employees. Bargaining then took place resulting in the creation of the 'social domain' working group, the tool that protected the advantages gained.

The next two phases, sadness and acceptance, existed in a very transitory and scarcely visible way. The players very quickly saw the positive aspects of the proposed change and, apart from a few isolated sadnesses associated with a restricted number of individual cases, acceptance was immediate, largely due I think to the participative approach.

23 Communication–metacommunication–overcommunication

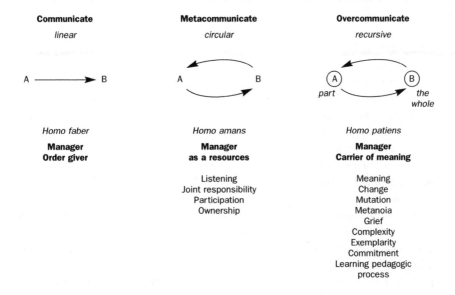

Figure 3.23a *Communicating: a complex process*

Among the changes in representation systems, there is the one that deals with communication, its function and its new forms. It affects all aspects of the organization and in particular the heads of communication. Roles change. The *homo faber*, the order giver, will be happy with a communication of linear causality. For the *homo amans*, the person of resources, communication consists of hearing and giving information. In addition, he or she knows the time required for the pedagogic processes and accompaniment, the need to 'communicate about the communication' in order to handle the relational processes and the transcultural problems.

The *homo patiens*, the managers who are carriers of meaning, knows that in addition they must 'over-communicate', that is, not only understand their interlocutors but also relocate the one-to-one exchanges in the context, in coherence and complexity. They must 'relocate the part in relation to the whole' and reposition all the exchanges in the logic of the common good.

> I have already said that we never communicate enough and, I repeat, never sufficiently face to face. Only 'physical' communication can transmit the meaning and the emotion and reassure the permanent questioning that a complex organization generates, especially during a period of change. For me it is a first priority of the manager.

24 The cursor: ambiguity and paradox of the change agent's role

As we see in Figure 3.24, on the one hand there is the logic and the order of delegation and control, the whole underpinned by McGregor's theory **X**. On the other hand, responsibility, trust and empowerment, the whole underpinned by theory **Y**.

As we have seen, the manager coach or the agent of change must at any moment move into a cursor position that is appropriate to the situation (development levels of the players, nature of the problem, degree of importance and urgency).

The ambiguity remains permanent because the order giver controller, manager or even union representative remains responsible to the end. But on the other side, from the start, the logic of subsidiarity can be initiated.

The problem will be for the two parties to accept on the one hand this unyielding ambiguity, and on the other the different positioning of the cursor without the 'freezer effect', by permanently finding the appropriate position. This will be the position that suits the situation and makes it possible for the players to develop. The paradox remains because the permanent task of the manager coach is to help others work things out for themselves, to 'spur them to take the initiative', to 'express themselves spontaneously'; so many paradoxical orders to be overcome.

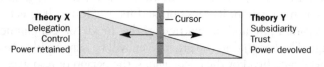

Figure 3.24 *The paradox and ambiguity of the role of accompaniment*

I discovered the mechanism of the cursor in a coaching session with Vincent Lenhardt. I find that it synthesizes remarkably well the way in which the managers of today and tomorrow must function. Wherever possible their behaviour should be based on trust, but they should not hesitate to return to control and the retaking of power where they deem it necessary. But beware, one must have a guide in order to be in one system rather than the other. In my case, I judge that I must preferably be in more than 90 per cent of situations in theory Y, leaving me therefore in a maximum of 10 per cent of cases the 'right' to take control or take a top-down decision.

This cursor theory must be widely publicized and explained internally, if it is not to cause useless frustration in teams who, while they normally function as is desirable in the world of trust, might be destabilized by a temporary return to control and authority.

25 The manager as a coach

The new dimension of management that leads order giver managers to become managers of resources and managers who are carriers of meaning, may be expressed by the term 'manager-coach'. In fact the order giver manager, who is both hierarchical decider and controller, must wear another hat; that of trainer, facilitator and enabler.

We call coaching any accompaniment made in the logic of a person regarding the other with the attitude of the trainer faced with a champion already fulfilled or with potential. This regard, which is carrier of the 'pygmalion' effect, is precisely the conviction that includes information, trust, support, encouragement, attention, 'modelling', and combines the protection and the permission that every human being needs, from youngest childhood to death, in order to develop fully on every plane.

In the professional sphere this function may be carried out by a consultant internal or external to the company, by any person in the company, even if he/she is not a coaching specialist of course, and even by the managers themselves in the presence of their colleagues. We shall discuss the latter case here.[18]

Throughout this book we have seen the considerable transformation of the identity, roles and skills of the players beyond technical competences, which is necessary in terms of values, representation systems, behaviours, aptitude to assume another degree of autonomy and to be carrier of this logic of co-responsibility.

These transformations that are as much individual as collective cannot be achieved unless the executives take the full role of accompanists or manager-coaches in addition to their role of order giver managers.

The two main axes of his role

The complexity of this role cannot be described in the present book. We shall simply highlight two major components:

1. Fish or rod.
In all cases the manager-coaches (MCs) will need to move the cursor between the following two poles:

- The problem brought by colleagues. The MCs intervene to solve the problem, suggest solutions, give examples, reframe the problem, 'get their hands dirty' with their colleagues. They give their colleagues the 'fish'.
- The colleagues who must find the solution themselves. The MCs intervene by focusing their colleagues' ability to find their own solution. They refuse to 'get their hands dirty', listen, question, manage, like Socrates, a true maieutic, give protection ('Take care with'), permission ('Good! Go ahead!') help in diagnosis, endorse the colleagues' decision. They help to fashion the rod. The two extremes are valuable, but most frequently the 'session' or the relation of coaching includes a positioning of the cursor that changes several times.

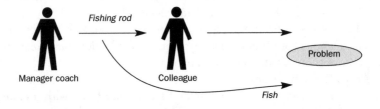

Figure 3.25a *Fish or fishing rod*

Does one provide a fish or a rod? On most occasions one needs to give a little of each and at the same time wherever possible move towards the building and the endorsement of the rod in order to empower the colleague.

2. Context and positioning
Most frequently, if the colleague comes with a problem and if the situation seems at first sight to be as simple as that shown in Figure 3.25b, all that the manager coach has to do, apart from what we have already said, and even more than the direct or indirect handling of the technical problem, is to locate the context in which the colleague and the problem lie and to help the colleague to position himself.

We believe that there are at least eight zones to be dealt with:

1. Am I, the manager-coach, the person to be seen? Am I competent or the good interlocutor? Am I not contaminated by such and such an element?

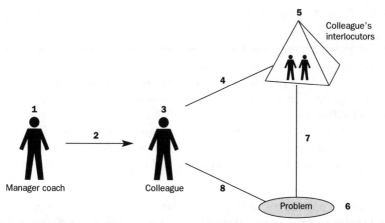

Figure 3.25b *The 'zones'*

2. Is our relationship 'healthy' or are there other psychological or institutional stakes at play? What is the real question? Our real relationship contract?
3. Is there a question of identity positioning for my colleague? Personal, professional or institutional? What is his identity problem?
4. What is the nature and quality of my colleague's relationship with the other parties involved in this problem (other services, hierarchy, suppliers, and so on)?
5. Who are the other interlocutors and what is our diagnosis of them?
6. What is the problem posed?
7. What relationship do the interlocutors have with the problem?
8. What relationship does my colleague have with the problem?

Generally, these eight questions in fact extend to many more and the repositioning work is more complex. But before getting his hands dirty with his colleagues, the manager-coach will help the latter to take a step back, take the questions one by one, pick out the blind spots, devise a broader plan of action, find out the wider or finer options, direct or indirect, in order to resolve the problem. The colleagues then come out of the coaching session seeing more clearly and no longer feeling alone.

We should note that this work described in an individual relationship can obviously be applied to a relationship with a team and becomes on the evidence even more complex to manage.

The ambiguity of the manager-coach

The great difference between the manager-coach and the internal or external coach lies in the fact of their managerial ambiguity: they are both trainers and bosses. They combine the roles of teachers and facilitators on the one hand, and on the other that of evaluators and controllers of the unavoidable sanctions of salary, bonus, career, and so on.

This ambiguity therefore has a major disadvantage. The manager-coaches do not possess the neutrality of trainers who are concerned only with the development of the persons concerned and offering room for a confidential word necessary to be able truly to show their weak points and to optimize the apprenticeship curve.

It does however have an advantage. The manager's coaches will be able to offer their colleagues operational jobs that will allow career progression towards a process that is both instructive and empowering.

The first example of the manager-coach that comes to mind, which is a good illustration of the ambiguity that you talk about, is that of Jean-René Fourtou offering to be my consultant on the SDM operation. His advice, as I have already explained, carries more weight than that of others, and pushes me to go further than I had done in another context. But he never gives me orders or instructions. He shares his experience with me with conviction and leaves me to take the decision; that is coaching.

When I find myself in the position of consultant, following a request from one of my colleagues, I will often say to him: 'I would not do this, but rather that, by exploring this or that avenue, and in any event the decision is yours'. I always try in such cases to base the advice that I give on a real-life experience rather than on a theory or a conviction, because this seems to leave more freedom of choice for the person who ultimately has to take the decision. Evidence is stronger than an order.

On the subject of individual coaching, there is also coaching a group of individuals. Meetings like these that were organized during the CEDEP training sessions are valuable occasions, enabling the involved manager to make the participants discover new aspects of management and, through questions, to become aware of new areas of freedom. During these exchanges which often touched on the SDM experience that the majority of the participants had lived through, I tried for example to show them how important it is for a senior executive to have assistants who have the courage to say no at certain times.

Urging managers to move away from a management through fear – which has affected us all and continues to affect the operation of businesses – towards a management through trust that authorizes everyone to give his opinion, seems to me to be the priority for coaching.

A number of failures, even business closures, might have been avoided if the management and employees had been able to express themselves other than through sly criticism of a decision which they knew only too well would lead to a catastrophe. This is what a generalized practice of coaching, at all levels in a company, ought to be able to end. But we are still a long from this, because the rare attempts that have been made here and there are generally too isolated, and very often overtaken by the 'freezer effect' due to uncontrolled behaviour that is totally at variance with the principles of coaching.

Notes

1 Tom Peters, *Thriving on Chaos*, New York: Knopf, 1987.

2 We refer the reader to the work of Michel Crozier, *L'Entreprise à l'Écoute*, Paris: InterÉditions, 1989, and in particular to the chapter on the principles of complex organizations. See also William Ouchi, *Théorie Z*, Paris: InterÉditions, 1982; reading this book led to the development of the concept of MSCE.

3 See Peter Senge and Alain Gauthier, *La Cinquième Discipline* (The Fifth Discipline), Paris: First, 1991.

4 Noël Tichy, *Control Your Destiny or Someone Else Will*, New York: Doubleday Currency, 1993.

5 We describe these concepts as basic because each of them would warrant lengthy development, examples and clarification; see V. Lenhardt, *Les Responsables Porteurs de Sens*, Paris: Insep, 1992. As an example, each of these concepts or diagrams merits several hours of theoretical development or work as group exercises in the Coaching and Teambuilding (C and T) training course for consultants over a period of 22 days that we hold at Transformance.

6 According to the formula of Hersey Blanchard and Dominique Tissier in *Le Management Situationnel*, Paris: INSEP, 1997.

7 Having no spinal column, the lobster only holds together thanks to its shell. Thus there are numerous managers who, because they are unsure of their own worth and have not acquired their 'ontological' security (the security of being), make use of their status and its attributes as an identity envelope, and are fearful of anything that might weaken it.

8 William Schutz, *The Human Element*, San Francisco: Jossey Bass, 1994.

9 See Emmanuel Faber, *Main Basse sur la Cité*, Paris: Hachette Littératures, 1992 and Alain Etchegoyen, *La Valse des Éthiques*, Paris: F. Bourin-Juillard, 1991.

10 Here we have rehearsed all the remarks on the danger of the removal of René Girard.

11 Cf. the phrase by Jacques Lacan quoted by his brother Marc François, a monk at Ganagobie: 'L'être ne naît que de la faille que produit l'étant de se dire'. Translated as: It is because I accept speaking of my injury that I let my mask and my defence system fall, and so accept myself in my weakness and my profound being.

12 Cf. Jean-Loup Dherse and Hugues Minguet, *L'Éthique ou le Chaos*, Paris: Presses de la Renaissance, 1998.

13 This is a reference to the classification of the great psychotherapist Victor Frankl. He distinguishes three classes: *homo faber* (artisan or expert), *homo amans* (relational being) and *homo patiens* (communion being capable of dying for his values).

14 Sumantra Goshal and Christopher Bartlett, *L'Entreprise Individualisée* (The Individualized Corporation), Paris: Maxima, 1998, p.16.

15 James C. Collins and Jerry I. Porras, *Built to Last*, op. cit.

16 Cf. the concepts of strokes, games, rackets in Vincent Lenhardt, *L'Analyse Transactionelle*, Paris: Retz, 1992.

17 Concerning the necessary technical and ethical reflection, for more details the reader is referred to the chapter 'The essential and the important hold sway' in *Oser la Confiance*, op. cit., and to the rules of the French Association of Coaching.

18 For more on the concept of coaching the reader is referred to *Les Responsables Porteurs de Sens* (op. cit.) which discusses the subject at length.

Conclusion

1 Three questions put to Vincent Lenhardt

Is the SDM operation repeatable?

It seems to me that this experience is certainly interesting as a challenging example for every manager. It is surely not a directly applicable methodology, but it may constitute an extremely stimulating and inspiring testimony as much at the level of values as for the positioning with regard to the stakes, the use of human beings to help the organization, the economics and the value creation, the many facets of this process, as well as the identity of the senior executives and the involvement of all associates.

Furthermore, although it is unique and set in a special context (that of a particular business, a large international French group, a world-wide set of problems, a context of specific players), it still remains quite similar to experiences gone through in other even larger groups (ABB or General Electric for example) or French companies of more modest size (for example the experience of the French subsidiary of Sulzer, put back on its feet by Bertrand Martin).

Personally, as the head of a consulting firm having accompanied more than fifty companies, large and small, in making more or less global changes during the past twenty years, after having attended and been received in numerous employers' associations, in academic departments and specialist institutes, and having become familiar with the different streams of management, I can truly testify that the action carried out by Alain Godard and his teams and associates adopts the direction and basic parameters that represent the important trends for management which have become necessary at the beginning of the twenty-first century. That is, to make every manager an entrepreneur, make them at the same time capable of working independently and in an 'across the board' way, and finally to lead the players and the organizations into permanent processes of reconfiguration and renewal.

Is this type of operation only possible in a time of crisis?

SDM was initiated in a period of crisis. It is certainly true that a crisis has the advantage of transforming gentle signals into strong messages and in this way forcing a group of players out of a denial of reality, making the frog want to jump out of the hot pan.

However, stress, fear and various pressures may paralyze the players or cause them to take refuge in attitudes that I would describe as regressive. For example, taking refuge in old remedies or reassuring oneself with the supposed certainty of figures, plans and battening down the hatches, leaving aside all the potential for creativity and true reconfiguration.

An approach of foresight can be more difficult to implement for the director, who is sometimes the only person to have the feeling of anticipation and to perceive the necessity of reconfiguring the second curve (cf. C. Handy). Others besides Alain Godard have been able to do it, such as for example the executives of General Electric and Monsanto with 180 degree turnarounds.

In the light of all these experiences, there seem to me to be two axes to be combined:

1. A dynamic based on an appeal to the players, and the building of a consistency of values in order to assist the value creation, because this dynamic is the source of a true lasting productiveness beyond one-off results.
2. A setting in motion that is not only the replacement of one obsolete curve with another, but the establishment of a cycle or a 'spiral' in the life of the company thus testifying to its now permanent reconfiguration process.

Is this experience and the conclusions that one can draw from it restricted only to the managers of international groups, or can they be useful to the proprietors of small businesses or small industrial companies?

The end of the twentieth century has seen the overwriting of the post-industrial era on the industrial era; everyone experiences the complexity, chaos and the contradictions that result. The risk is great for a society that is moving at two speeds, where the rich become richer and the less favoured suffer from exclusion. For this reason the business world with its crises and its difficulties paradoxically represents a universe to which people cling compared with the other institutions that are often even more at a loss: the civil service, schools, the family, religious institutions, unions, political parties, and so on. The company has become an important place beyond its economic aims. Being a place for training, discussion and membership, it now also offers, increasingly, a space for the building of people and a space for socialization.

Understanding the new dynamic of this empowerment of the players, learning the way into modernity, the life of networks, employability, working on a group project, acquiring competences and ontological security as compared with the lobster complex, and so on, all this becomes central, not only for small businesses and small industrial companies, but also for very small businesses. In an age where each individual can create a global single person business in his bedroom with just a fax machine, a PC and an Internet connection, the experience that we have commented upon and the concepts that enable the components of a new managerial identity to be defined seem to us to be useful for everyone who wishes to become a manager in the world today.

2 Advice from Alain Godard

First of all, it seems to me essential to recognize that if the type of solution represented by the SDM experience must be implemented every time that the conditions are appropriate – that is, more often than one might think – certain situations sometimes require the company to adopt more conventional and harsher restructuring operations. One must then have the courage – a quality that is necessary in every case – to carry out these operations while respecting the values of the company and the interests of the people involved. I have done it in the past and will do it in the future if necessary.

To return to SDM, the reader will know more about how teams and individuals behave than I did at the time. I hope that this is an advantage. So far as I am concerned, having neither a model nor solid theoretical foundations, the SDM experience was built by progressing from the observations that had formed my own convictions, from my experience and from the support of the participating co-developers. I believe that these words – convictions, experience, co-development – are the key factors for the success of the operation.

This not the kind of operation to embark upon if one does not hold strong convictions that one has the solution to the problem. It is these convictions that generate the required energy and courage to lead the operation.

This is not the kind of approach to adopt without experience at a general level or in the specific field in question. To the extent that it runs counter to the traditional solutions, it demands the permanent 'protection' that experience can provide, and knowledge of the terrain, the environment and the people who surround it.

This is not the route to take for anyone who is not at heart prepared to work transparently, share his feelings, strengths and weaknesses, listen, and treat others as his equals, as men like himself. The shared vision, the adoption of the project and then its co-development can only be achieved at this price.

This book is first of all intended for those who are convinced that ready-made solutions have their limitations, that human richness and potential are largely unexploited in our companies, and that the economic and the social nourish one another and cannot be separated.

I hope that such people, if they find themselves in an appropriate environment, will not hesitate to engage in such a process, adapting the ideas and solutions that we have proposed to their own contexts. For this book does not claim to be a model, but much more food for thought and a stimulus to action to make our businesses more effective. If it helps to guide enough managers towards a new approach, in order to generate the necessary critical mass to make something truly new occur in many companies, then it will have done more than achieve its *objectives*, leaving room for *hope* and opening the door to *dreams*.

Appendix: Management Questionnaire

For readers interested in an analysis and a deeper understanding of the 'management questionnaire' this Appendix contains the full text.

We remind the reader that this tool which was developed by one of the working parties (see pages 21–22) is used both to measure and to improve the behaviour of the hierarchies in relation to the values and management principles subscribed to by the company.

Simplify, decentralize, manage

At its reorganization, the Agro sector defined the framework in which it wished to achieve its ambitions and improve its results. The behaviour of managers, in all units throughout the world, is one of the key elements of its success.

The management questionnaire is the tool chosen to measure the progress achieved by each manager in applying the principles and values of the sector *vis-à-vis* the members of his team who report to him directly.

The following outcomes are expected from this questionnaire:

- Establishment of trust;
- Strengthening of team cohesion;
- Sharing of the vision, the values and the principles for action by the sector especially:
  – constant attention for the client;
  – development of autonomy, initiative and responsibility as a whole.

The tool itself

It is a measurement of progress that the manager requests from his immediate colleagues. These colleagues are a particular form of client. A more objective knowledge of their perceptions and expectations is a prerequisite to the advancement in the manager's performance with his team. Coincidentally with creating a favourable climate for change, the manager has data that enable him to improve. It is not a tool for personal judgement. It is not a performance review of managers carried out by their colleagues in order to inform their superiors. The results are not used for individual discussion or assessment of the mastery of a post.

The questionnaire was prepared by a working party within the framework of the SDM project and tested in a pilot operation by eleven managers and their teams in France.

The questions exemplify the practices of management, especially those that the sector wishes to see developed. The manager asks his immediate subordinates for their perception of his personal application of these principles (the replies are confidential and anonymous). He undertakes to take action by defining a plan of campaign with them.

This questionnaire is designed to be common to all units in the sector throughout the world and will eventually be rounded off with some specific questions.

The RP Group and then the sector have defined the framework in which the units that go to make them up must evolve in the form of 'principles for action'.

Managers must share these principles with their teams and make them live them out in their daily actions.

The questionnaire is the tool chosen by each manager in order to advance, both individually and with his colleagues.

Who uses it?

The first test was carried out by a volunteer group of managers including the managing director of the sector and head office supervisors. This test enabled the questionnaire and feedback process to be improved. It will be extended by stages down the hierarchical levels in order to secure its progressive approval in France and abroad. The objective is to extend use of this tool in 1995 to the majority of managers in the sector.

How is it used?

The manager's immediate colleagues fill in the questionnaire and send it in a sealed envelope to the person in charge of the operation. Anonymity is guaranteed. Everyone can express himself as he wishes, either face to face with his manager, or collectively at the feedback meeting.

It is preferable to stipulate a short period for completion of the questionnaire (ten days maximum).

Processing of the results

Calculation of average per subject

Individual replies

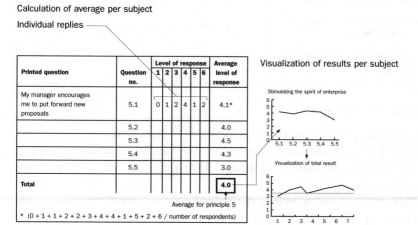

After processing the questions, the analysis of the results will be sent in a sealed envelope to the manager. They contain the average of the responses to each question as well as the distribution of the replies.

These results are the property of the manager who has the right to decide on the type of publication that he wishes to give them. They will form the basis of the exchanges between the manager and his team at the feedback meeting.

The calculation is produced in the following way:

- For each reply we count the number of instances of 'agree' and 'don't agree', numbered 1 to 6;
- A table is drawn up that allows a graph to be drawn for each principle (7) as well as a synthesis chart.

This operation does not allow individual responses to be found. If there are fewer than four replies for a manager, it is not possible to obtain any results.

Unfolding the process

The process is managed by the head of Human Resources in liaison with an external consultant who will ensure the quality of the operation. He will also guarantee the anonymity and confidentiality of the replies.

Operations	Manager	Manager's immediate staff	Management of process	Timetable (D = Day)
• Provision of coded questionnaire on request of manager			○	
• Launch meeting				D
• Distribution of questionnaires to participants	○			
• Completion of questionnaires and delivery to Human Resources Dept. for processing of replies		○		D + 10
• Compilation and transmission of results to manager			○	D + 20
• Feedback of results from manager to his/her team	○			D + 30
• Action plan				

Positioning of the tool

The SDM project recognized the driving role of management in conducting change. This occurs through the development of the relationship between the manager and the managed, measured with the aid of the questionnaire that we put to you.

This measurement completes the economic indicators already introduced and makes it possible to obtain a global view of the piloting of the company

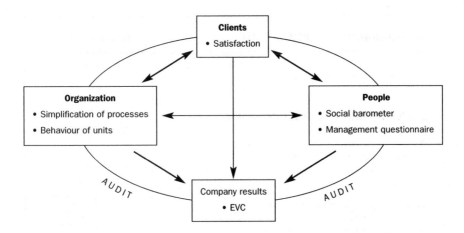

in terms of results. Such results should derive from the will of the sector to advance in its management of people, in the simplification of processes and in the satisfaction of its clients.

What do others do?

The use of a questionnaire concerning the relation between a manager and his colleagues has been experimented with in various cultural contexts. In each case, it is based on a vision of the business.

For example, this tool is widely used in France at Rank-Xerox in a form quite similar to that which we propose. The manager fills in the form himself and compares his self-evaluation with that of his colleagues. At the end of the discussion between the manager and his team a plan of internal action is recorded.

Closer to us, a team of the Agro sector has used, as part of the development of the total quality programme, a management questionnaire aimed at 'creating a favourable environment'.

Confidentiality has always been maintained as a matter of principle. In all cases, this tool has been viewed as a tool of progress for the managers with their teams. In certain circumstances, it may be used in order to understand better the quality of less directly hierarchical or 'across the board' relations (projects, for example).

MANAGEMENT QUESTIONNAIRE

MANAGER CODE ⬚⬚⬚

Reply to each question by entering a number 1–6. Number 1 signifies 'definitely disagree'; number 6 signifies 'completely agree'.

1. GIVE PRIORITY TO THE CUSTOMER

Our clients are our *raison d'être*. We must constantly listen to them, anticipate their needs, and provide them with total quality responses.

Q1.1 My manager asks me to get to know our clients

Q1.2 My manager asks me to know the needs of our clients

Q1.3 My manager asks me to measure the satisfaction of our clients

Q1.4 The satisfaction of my clients is taken into account in the evaluation of my performance

1	2	3	4	5	6

2. FACILITATE INDIVIDUAL DEVELOPMENT

Each manager must aim to facilitate development of the competences of his colleagues and their career progression. He must establish a climate of trust and reciprocal candour and encourage expression and dialogue.

Q2.1 My manager is available for everyone and for the team

Q2.2 My manager listens to what people say to him

Q2.3 My manager acknowledges work achieved

Q2.4 My manager establishes a climate of trust

Q2.5 My manager sees to the training of his colleagues

Q2.6 My manager offers me aid and assistance

Q2.7 My manager discusses with me points that need to be improved

Q2.8 My manager entrusts me with projects that allow me to develop my strong points

Q2.9 My manager transfers his expertise to his colleagues

1	2	3	4	5	6

3. CULTIVATE SPECIFICITY

Each entity and every manager must pursue the practice of his occupation and adopt the most effective organization for his domain of activity.

	1	2	3	4	5	6
Q3.1 My manager ensures that the specific features of our occupation are acknowledged within the company						
Q3.2 My manager adapts the organization of his unit to the specific features of our occupation						
Q3.3 My manager has a plan of action to increase our performance in the exercise of our occupation						

4. SAFEGUARD THE INTERESTS OF THE GROUP

Each person, in every decision and action, must take into account not only the interests of his own field of activity, but also the more general interests of the Group.

	1	2	3	4	5	6
Q4.1 My manager asks us to take our decisions while safeguarding the interests of the RP Group						
Q4.2 My manager regularly provides information about the life of the RP Group and the Agro sector						
Q4.3 My manager takes into account in his actions the company's values of security and the environment						
Q4.4 My manager encourages me to use at equal cost the internal means and resources of the RP Group and the Agro sector						
Q4.5 When there is a vacancy to be filled, my manager gives preference to internal recruitment from the Agro sector and the RP Group						
Q4.6 My manager attaches importance to the image that his team reflects to the RP Group						

5. STIMULATE ENTREPRENEURSHIP

The organization and management style must, at every level, facilitate individual and collective initiatives and encourage innovation in all areas.

	1	2	3	4	5	6
Q5.1 My manager encourages me to make new proposals						
Q5.2 My manager helps me to implement proposals, even if that implies a portion of risk						
Q5.3 When I make a mistake, my manager gives me constructive advice						
Q5.4 My manager acknowledges individual and collective successes						
Q5.5 My manager encourages the development of partnerships with other parts of the company or with external clients						

6. APPLY THE PRINCIPLE OF EMPOWERMENT

Whatever can be perfectly well carried out at a given level must not be taken over by a higher level. Everyone must be assured that each of his colleagues has the necessary means for his mission.

	1	2	3	4	5	6
Q6.1 My manager defines with me the responsibilities that he entrusts me with						
Q6.2 My manager respects the autonomy that he has delegated						
Q6.3 My manager takes responsibility for the decisions taken by his colleagues						
Q6.4 My manager facilitates access to all information relating to everyone's work						
Q6.5 My manager delegates the maximum tasks possible according to the abilities of his team						
Q6.6 When he delegates, my manager takes time to explain the objectives						
Q6.7 My manager is able to say what is going well						
Q6.8 My manager is able to say what is not going well						

7. BE PERSONALLY COMMITTED

All consultation prior to decision must be genuine. Everyone, in all his deeds, is personally committed and assumes responsibility for his decisions. He watches over the information of the people involved.

	1	2	3	4	5	6
Q7.1 My manager consults his team before taking a decision						
Q7.2 When my manager asks for my opinion, he has not yet taken a decision						
Q7.3 My manager informs the persons concerned about decisions						
Q7.4 My manager ensures that each decision is followed by a clear plan of action that is implemented quickly						
Q7.5 My manager takes into account the social aspect, as well as the technical and economic aspects in his decisions						
Q7.6 When he takes a decision my manager takes care to respect people and their diversity						
Q7.7 When he takes a decision my manager takes responsibility for the consequences.						

Index